CLUES
W9-CBC-200

THE DEVIL WITH JAMES BOND!

The Devil with James Bond!

BY ANN S. BOYD

JOHN KNOX PRESS
Richmond, Virginia

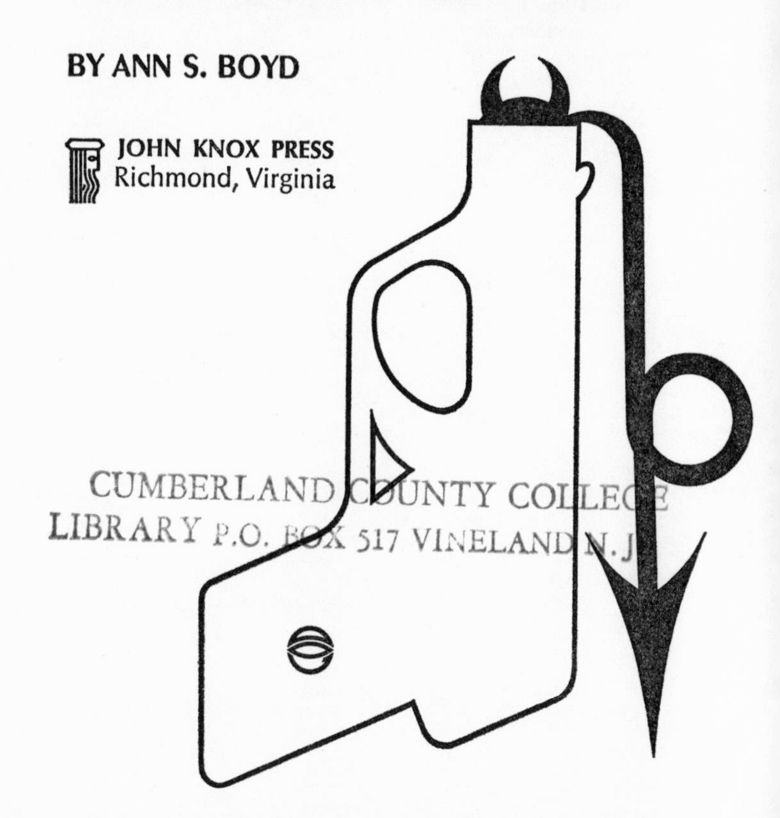

Unless otherwise noted, Scripture quotations are from the *Revised Standard Version of the Bible,* copyrighted 1946 and 1952.

Grateful acknowledgment is made to the Christian Century Foundation, who originally published "James Bond: Modern-day Dragonslayer" (May 19, 1965). Quotations from *Casino Royale, Live and Let Die, Moonraker, Diamonds Are Forever, Doctor No,* and *Goldfinger* are used by permission of The Macmillan Company; from *Thunderball* by permission of The Viking Press; from *You Only Live Twice, The Man with the Golden Gun,* and *On Her Majesty's Secret Service* by permission of The New American Library, Inc.

LIBRARY OF CONGRESS CATALOG CARD NUMBER: 67-10605

PRINTED IN THE UNITED STATES OF AMERICA
J. 3672

Dedication

To Dick and the children—
Nancy, Janet, John, and Laura—
who suffered through a year of
"bond-age" with me.

And to our parents, who trusted
that no news was good news!

PREFACE

It is somewhat ironic to admit that this book is the result of having gone to see the movie *Goldfinger* last year as a break between semesters in my work as a graduate student at Drew University.

What had begun as an evening's relaxation to celebrate having completed two seminar reports soon resulted in months of free-lance research—all because my initial reaction to the movie was that James Bond was like a modern version of a knight. Since I was anxious to compare the contemporary adventures of secret agent 007 with the various aspects of medieval knighthood, I began buying and rereading the Fleming books in chronological order.

The way I began was probably the best way to read Bond—sitting up all night on a hot, crowded, stuffy coach train going cross-country in bad weather after my plane flight had been grounded. By the time my silent seat companion had shifted into the seventh yoga-like position trying to find some combination in which to stay asleep, I was off in Fleming's "never-never-land" and even regretted the train's arrival in New York City. By that time I had discovered the chapter on evil in *Casino Royale* and the word "accidie" in Mister Big's first speech in *Live and Let Die,* and the hunt was on. A month later I found Fleming's foreword to *The Seven Deadly Sins,* which served as a convincing argument for me that Ian Fleming had indeed had a great deal more in mind when he began his "spy story to end all spy stories" than he had originally admitted. Soon my part-time fascination grew into a full-time preoccupation (as much as my family and other responsibilities allowed). My initial questions soon grew into an article in *The Christian Century:* "James Bond: Modern-day Dragon-slayer," and the article into this book.

In a way the structure of the book follows a pattern created by the questions which the Bond phenomenon raised and the subsequent answers revealed by research. It alternates from synthesis to analysis and back to synthesis again: first by seeing the Bond series as a whole in relation to the imagery of St. George and the dragon; then by breaking down this imagery into its various aspects within the context of what I have termed our "syncopated society"—in the image of the secret agent and in the tremendous problem of apathy seen from both sociological and theological perspectives; and finally by bringing these elements back together in a historical context, moving from fiction into fact in the real-life figure of Dietrich Bonhoeffer.

Since this book is more like a honeycomb than a spider's web, I have tried to acknowledge whenever possible those scholars and writers whose research in depth have contributed the "honey" to this cross-disciplinary study.

My special appreciation goes to those faculty members at Drew University in Madison, New Jersey, whose support has been a continual source of encouragement: Professors Nelle Morton, John Godsey, Robert Friedrichs, and James Ranck. All responsibility for my somewhat novel hypotheses must rest upon my own shoulders, however. In addition, I should like to thank staff members of libraries at Drew and Summit, New Jersey, as well as many local bookdealers, for their assistance in helping me locate reference materials. I should also mention the fact that the critical support which Kingsley Amis gave to Ian Fleming in his *James Bond Dossier* has served to reinforce my own opinions.

Finally, I would like to comment that it seems to me that men must be able to write more books than women because they have both secretaries and wives. In my case, since I had neither, my particular appreciation must go to Ruth Jenkins for her unfailing assistance in our household; to my husband, for his willingness to share his escape reading material with me and for his forbearance above and beyond the call of duty; and to our children, who have learned to cope with an unusual sibling rival—"mother's book!"

Ann S. Boyd
Summit, New Jersey

CONTENTS

THE DEVIL WITH JAMES BOND!

001 · Introduction: "Slug It Apathy"

MATTHEW 24:12
"And because *anomia* shall abound, the love
of many shall wax cold." (K.J.V.)
"As lawlessness spreads, men's love for
one another will grow cold." (N.E.B.)

It was three-twenty in the morning, a cold March morning, as a small red Fiat turned off a dark, quiet suburban street into a railroad parking lot.

Its driver, a slight dark-haired woman of twenty-eight, was tired after her evening's work as manager of a bar. As she wearily got out of her car and started toward the back entrance which would lead to the safety of her second-floor apartment in the adjacent building, the movements of a man on the far side of the parking lot caught her eye.

Immediately alert to the risk of possible danger and doubly aware of the dark, empty street, she changed direction, heading instead toward the front of the building and the police call box up on the corner. Her heels clicked staccato-like up the slight incline, faster and faster as she realized that the man actually was following her.

The distance closed between them. She started to run, past the drugstore, the cleaners, but her pursuer caught up with her under the streetlight by a bookstore. A shrill scream pierced the heavy winter silence of the night, "Oh, my God, he stabbed me! Please help me! Please help me!"

Windows flew open, a few heads appeared cautiously from

behind the drawn blinds and shades in the apartment building across the street. A man hollered, "Let that girl alone!" The attacker withdrew, fading into the darkness, heading toward a white sedan down the street.

Disoriented by the attack, anxious to treat her wounds, perhaps naïvely trusting that in some way the observers watching from across the street somehow would be able to guarantee her safe journey home, the girl headed back down the street, around the corner of the drugstore next to the parking lot.

But the assailant had only faked his retreat, circling around instead in the darkness, perhaps hiding between the cars. Suddenly he pounced out at her, stabbing her again and again. Her screams rang out a second time, "I'm dying! I'm dying!"

This time windows flew open in the apartment house on the other side of the parking lot. Horrified observers were able to see the man actually run off to the white sedan and drive away. The girl continued, slowly, haltingly on around the building. She was able to crawl past the first door, but then realized that she could not possibly reach the safety of her own doorway farther down the block. Somehow she managed to open the second door, only to collapse at the bottom of the stairs. No one had come to her assistance.

But the attacker was able to track her down again. This time his assault was instantly fatal. Catherine Genovese was dead.

The police who arrived minutes later were too late to help. They could only begin to assemble the astounding story of what had happened. One man, the one neighbor who had finally called the police, admitted that his delay had been the result of his not wanting to get involved.

One by one the New York police were able to count up thirty-eight witnesses who had seen and known what was happening, yet had done nothing—ordinary citizens who had awakened, looked out their windows, and then, not wanting to get involved, had gone back to sleep. One had yelled out of his window; one had finally called the police, but not until after the girl had died.

No one had gone to her immediate assistance, yet in the weeks following her murder, the reports of the Catherine Genovese case attracted city-wide and then national attention. Soon the reports of the brutal murder and the search for the assailant were actually bypassed in the astonishment over the inaction of the witnesses. In a moment of dreadful clarity, one woman's horrified response spoke for all, "Dear God, what have we come to!"

The next reaction was a search for some explanation. Various suggestions were made and various targets were hit, such as the inadequacy of the police force and the lack of a special emergency call number. But although fear of involvement had been the first rationalization, it remained for the newspaper editor, A. M. Rosenthal, to diagnose the illness as more severe: "For in that instant of shock, the mirror showed quite clearly what was wrong, that the face of mankind was spotted with the disease of apathy—all mankind. But this was too frightening a thought to live with and soon the beholders began to set boundaries for the illness, to search frantically for causes that were external and to look for the carrier."[1]

Psychologists, sociologists, theologians, and psychiatrists could add little except qualifying terms for the syndrome. The Genovese case immediately became the focal point for a continuing series of news items, soon stereotyped and blunted by their repetition under the editors' designation, *"Slug it apathy!"* As soon as what had happened could be pigeonholed, it became easier to ignore, and the original shock faded into the general pattern of concern over the state of contemporary society.

For while theologians ponder their "hermeneutical" tasks and ministers prepare "honest-to-God" sermons, the "world come of age" often appears to the average layman quite like an obscure package wrapped in brown paper, sitting on his mail table and ticking. Will it blow up in his face at the least provocation like a time bomb regardless of how he might try to prevent it? Or, if he leaves it alone, will it just run down like a clock without winding, "not with a bang, but a whimper"?

The old, sentimental image of the traditional "little brown church in the dell" as spiritual hub of a cohesive community has been shattered by changing political, economic, and sociological conditions, but a new image of the mission and responsibility of the church in an age of ambiguity has not yet been formed.

Social historians may some day be able to decide if the syncopated society in which we live may be more aptly designated the "twisted age" because of the strange contorted dances of the younger generation, or the "wistful" age, because, as Ernest Becker observed, "Never before had so many seen man's shortcomings so clearly and been able to do so little about them." We have left the stage of a primitive savage society in which men existed as little better than other animals, only to reach a more tragic dimension in which a man's market value depends upon the value of the machine which could replace him.

Because it suggests elision and the offbeat, the term "syncopation" provides an excellent descriptive term for the society in which we participate. First of all, as Webster's dictionary indicates, in music "syncopation" is the "temporary displacing or shifting of the regular metrical accent." In grammar the "syncope" is the "loss or elision of one or more sounds from the middle of a word (as in ne'er for never)." But, secondly, and much more suggestively, in medicine the "syncope," which comes from a Greek word meaning "a cutting up," means a "swoon due to cerebral anemia." Appropriately our times have been termed "out of joint" and our apathy is the long swoon from which we need reviving.

Although in music syncopation is very enjoyable, in a society syncopation can have disastrous results. Socially we observe syncopation whenever institutions persist long after their ability to function as required, when new institutions do not appear in time to meet the demands of new situations, and when individuals are left to grapple with such situations without cultural support. Today myriads of objective analyses document the extent of man's inability to cope with a society which has developed faster than its powers to handle all of its needs. Other projective studies suggest that the problems we have now are simple compared to the new ethical and moral questions which are about to be raised by forthcoming medical and technical discoveries. The results of this syncopation are manifested directly in the many portrayals of men and women in various states of "eclipse"—by dope, alcohol, mental and emotional illnesses, criminal and civil disobedience.

This elision has been described in split-level dimensions by philosophers and social scientists as well as by the creative artists: first of all, as the loss of the self, delineated in such books as Viktor Frankl's *Man's Search for Meaning,* Allen Wheelis' *The Quest for Identity,* and Helen Merrell Lynd's *On Shame and the Search for Identity*; second, the loss of community, as described by Maurice Stein in his *Eclipse of Community*; and third, the loss of the transcendent, which has been presented not only by Martin Buber in his *Eclipse of God,* but also by the young theologians who are currently proclaiming the "death of God."

It has remained, however, for the artist and the poet to express this sense of loss most poignantly and personally. The movement in art over the last century from realism through impressionism into symbolism and surrealism presents the visual analogue for William Butler Yeats's lines:

> Things fall apart; the centre cannot hold;
> Mere anarchy is loosed upon the world,
> The blood-dimmed tide is loosed, and everywhere
> The ceremony of innocence is drowned;
> The best lack all conviction, while the worst
> Are full of passionate intensity.[2]

The emptiness, sterility, misery, and solitude of modern man lost in a strange world of the machine and the atom has been captured directly in Giacometti's "sculpture of despair" and such faces as those in paintings by George Tooker ("The Subway") or Edvard Munch ("The Cry"). Surrealism illustrates the questioning of values in an age of ambiguity, and even the pop art of the day echoes W. H. Auden's line: "God will cheat no one, not even the world of its triumph."[3]

The most outstanding single characteristic of our present syncopated society, however, is that it has become confused about, and even lost, its "beat," for it exists under the perilous dichotomy of dualistic thinking, a state which John MacMurray terms the "desire to know the truth without having to live by the truth." A parallel description of this characteristic as it affects a specific situation has been provided by the Pulitzer prize-winning journalist, Harrison Salisbury, in his book, *The Shook-Up Generation*: "We have gangs not because we do not know how to prevent them, but because we do not have enough interest or energy to do the things we already know will bring an end to delinquency. We do not lack knowledge. We lack the will."[4]

Part of this confusion about the "beat," however, is that even when our intentions have been the very finest, the results have brought about unforeseen disaster. It is a devastating experience to realize that we have actually increased human misery, suffering, and hunger by giving to the needy, healing the sick, and feeding the hungry as we face the population explosion now taking place around the world. Perhaps one of the best capsule descriptions of man in the twentieth century has been provided by psychologist Erik Erikson, who wrote:

> Artful perverter of joy and keen exploiter of strength, man is the animal that has learned to survive "in a fashion," to multiply without food for the multitudes, to grow up healthily without reaching personal maturity, to live well but without purpose, to invent ingeniously without aim, and to kill grandiosely without need.[5]

Just like the farmer confronting the state agricultural expert who had invited him to a workshop on advanced farming techniques, we might also admit that we are not now "farming" as well as we already know how to "farm." And the tragic partner to this realization is that all too often we just do not care enough to try. With Ecclesiastes too often we might say, "All things are full of weariness; a man cannot utter it; the eye is not satisfied with seeing, nor the ear filled with hearing." Neither church nor society has yet been able to cope with the discontinuities of change, the elision of human values, and the consequences of transition from poverty to affluence, from daily toil to automation, from ignorance to technical competence, from fear of the future to hope for the present. It is easier for astronauts to meet each other's space capsules 180 miles above the earth traveling at 17,500 miles per hour than it is for presidents of cold-war nations to meet each other around a peace table. We are beset daily by a variety of small demons; the demonic lurks behind every headline.

But suddenly out of the swirling gray mists of contemporary ambiguity regarding the nature and worth of mankind, a mysterious figure has appeared. Is he a modern Perseus armed by the gods in order to slay Medusa? St. George on a white horse on his way to kill a dragon? Don Quixote in search of windmills? Christian of *Pilgrim's Progress* traveling through the Slough of Despond or imprisoned in the castle of Giant Despair?

No, none of these exactly, but a figure uniquely appropriate to the modern idiom: Commander James Bond, the incredible British undercover agent 007, created by the imagination of the late novelist Ian Fleming, whose phenomenal popularity brings a host of questions to the surface:

Does James Bond have any more or any less theological significance than the comic strip *Peanuts*?

Why are his fantastic exploits attracting record-setting motion picture audiences as well as millions of people around the world who read of them in more than eighteen different languages?

What accounts for the astonishing variety of critical comments, both among the earlier critics and among those presently seeking more esoteric reasons for the series' popularity?

Although it has been reported publicly that Fleming himself regarded his work as mere "piffle" and that he "deliberately intended it to be exciting, successful, lucrative and, as he scornfully remarked, not in the least 'literary,' "[6] can we find perhaps in the Bond series a twentieth-century layman's deliberate analysis of the relationship between the "demonic" and individual responsibility?

Might we suspect that James Bond speaks to us as significantly as his analogues (Perseus, St. George, Don Quixote, Christian) spoke to their contemporaries centuries ago?

Just what is the Bond phenomenon anyway?

To answer these questions we shall have to follow a few wandering trails, even scurrying out into the bushes occasionally to snag a few pertinent points from various disciplines, ranging from literature, through psychology and sociology, even into theology and art. But with Bond for a guide, even the bushes might prove inviting!

002 • "Things Are Not What They Seem"

"You see the ways the fisherman doth take
To catch the fish, what engines doth he make?
Behold! how he engageth all his wits,
Also his snares, lines, angles, hooks and nets.
Yet fish there be that neither hook nor line
Nor snare nor net nor engine can make thine;
They must be groped for and be tickled, too,
Or they will not be catch'd whate're you do."
"The Author's Apology for His Book"
John Bunyan

Would you believe me if I said that James Bond is one of the most famous mythological heroes of all time?

No? Well, would you believe James Bond is one of the seven greatest legendary champions of Christendom?

NO? Well, would you believe James Bond is the greatest secret agent in the world of fiction?

Maybe? Well, then perhaps you'll settle for the James Bond adventures being a lot of fun and great escape reading material?

You would? Good. At least we can begin together somewhere!

You see, the difficulty in all this business of trying to discuss the Bond phenomenon is that it's very hard to take the whole affair very seriously, especially when Fleming never would himself. So, we have to start out on the surface of things, and wait to see what develops.

A note of warning to the reader before we begin, however:

Don't try to read any of the Bond adventures seriously! To read Bond as a scholastic exercise surely would smack of what's been termed "comic incommensurability." Bond was meant for fun, for escape, and legitimately requires the "willing suspension of disbelief"! Just like the fairy tale of the princess and the pea, real literary critics can't sleep very well when they try to read Fleming just like they'd read James Joyce. If Fleming was interested in what Kierkegaard termed "indirect communication," the least we can do is to read him the way he intended! The only real value in rereading Fleming is to discover that there is more to his series of thriller adventures than one originally might suspect. The more one reads him, the more one may appreciate his work and regret the distortion which the "Bondomania" of the movies has produced.

Regardless of what anyone says now and whatever significance people might consider the Bond phenomenon to have a century from now, there can be little doubt concerning the impact it made when it struck the cultural mainland with full-fledged hurricane force in the 1960's. The ubiquitous symbol of secret agent 007 was found everywhere—from bread and bubblegum to men's fashions and toiletries, from parlor games to children's dolls and paper dolls, from his own image to that of imitations in books, films, and television series. More than two hundred commercial products were authorized to carry the official trademark, while hundreds of others hitched onto the Bond-wagon surreptitiously. The James Bond syndrome was soon a universal focal-point for countless Walter Mittys. As Kingsley Amis said, "We don't want to have Bond to dinner, or go golfing with Bond, or talk to Bond. We want to be Bond!"

The results of this gold rush were a million times more lucrative for its investors than California gold-seekers ever could have dreamed. "Million" soon became a commonplace adjective anywhere the Bond-touch was felt: Ian Fleming himself became a millionaire before his death in 1964; actor Sean Connery, who really *was* Bond for the movie audiences, was soon able to command a million dollars per film himself. By the spring of 1966 the sales of the books had reached forty-five million copies, with more than one hundred million movie tickets having been sold.

The hordes of critics soon appeared. Before the last Fleming novel, two full-length books analyzing the secret agent's activities were published, and three more about Bond and Fleming followed within a year.[1] Book reviewers and commentators were running right along with the pack. Their opinions ranged from those who viewed Bond primarily as an all-powerful hero figure a la Jung (Claude Mauriac), a bungler (Russell Baker), or a dull uninteresting man in himself, a simple *pro forma* (Amis), to those who attributed his audience appeal to voyeurism (Jacques Barzun), to the Freudian "latency period" (Cyril Connolly), to a longing for the defeat of modern gadgetry, viz., the Bomb (Mauriac again), or—even more remarkably—to Goldwater's conservative mystique (the *New Guard,* published by the Young Americans for Freedom).[2] As a critic, Anthony Boucher continued to maintain that he had never been able to understand the appeal of the Fleming books, and writers Margery Allingham and John Le Carré concurred in their disapproval. Intuitively they recognized that in some peculiar way the books of Bond do not quite properly belong in their field.

In the meantime, back on the newsstands and the box office, the general public continued to demonstrate its approval financially. Could it be that the James Bond phenomenon had become simply a case of the "emperor's new clothes"? Was it just another symptom of the playboy mentality of the pepsi generation? If so, P. T. Barnum's injunction continues in force; if not, the phenomenon deserves more serious consideration.

Given the "hula-hoop" type of evidence already demonstrated, it might seem preposterous to suggest that the James Bond phenomenon has any deep literary, sociological, or theological value. But, with the deliberate intention of being a little preposterous and of trying to provoke discussion, I shall continue my hypothesis that whereas *Peanuts* (whose relevance has been championed by Robert L. Short)[3] is speaking to the "children" in a "world come of age," the series of Bond novels is directly relevant to "adolescents" searching for values and for a hero figure, one who would defend justice and humanity. And, despite the distortions of

Fleming's original materials in the films, their immediate appeal as "highly sophisticated comic strips for adults" has revealed that the Fleming formula was applicable to the general public as well as the original reading market.

This hypothesis rests on the contention that the James Bond phenomenon has contained a literary time bomb which could not have been detected until the entire series was completed and all the data compiled. The insight which the German satirist Kurt Tucholsky enjoined upon his readers and which Peter Berger echoes is applicable here: "Things are not what they seem. They are different. Quite, quite different." In later chapters we shall attempt to discover just why the entire Western world seems caught on Bond-fire, but here we begin with the material itself.

Perhaps the best criterion for understanding the Bond phenomenon from a literary standpoint, morally and technically, was provided by Edgar Allan Poe in the words he supplied his detective Dupin in "The Purloined Letter":

> There is a game of puzzles . . . which is played upon a map. One party playing requires another to find a given word—the name of town, river, state, or empire—any word, in short, upon the motley and perplexed surface of the chart. A novice in the game generally seeks to embarrass his opponents by giving them the most minutely lettered names; but the adept selects such words as stretch, in large characters, from one end of the chart to the other. These, like the over-largely lettered signs and placards of the street, escape observation by dint of being excessively obvious; and here the physical oversight is precisely analogous with the moral inapprehension by which the intellect suffers to pass unnoticed those considerations which are too obtrusively and too palpably self-evident.[4]

In a similar manner, by stretching his intentions over a series of thirteen novels following the pattern of the thriller genre, Fleming has been able to utilize a variety of literary and theological insights without detection. The casual reader of one or two books in the series is exposed to only a fraction of the total content. However, a careful analysis of the completed work reveals it as the saga of a modern knight of faith whose adventures involve a gallery of modern demons which have been attacking contemporary mankind just as diabolically as Medusa and all the other legendary demons and dragons attacked mankind in ages past. Rather than casting pearls before swine, Fleming's genius has cast swine as the personifications of the devil before a hero who is willing to sacrifice all for the great pearl of life and faith.

Individually the Bond adventures parody the form of the detective thrillers: secret agent 007 proceeds to seek out and destroy various adversaries, each of which surpasses its predecessor in the manner of diabolic test or ordeal he presents for Bond to endure. The basic *modus operandi* of each novel is the same: (1) 007's call to duty by "M," head of the secret service bureau; (2) his voluntary acceptance of the mission; (3) a period of reconnaissance and preparation which culminates in 007's personal involvement and commitment to the task; (4) the encounter with the adversary, with the nature of the particular evil he represents spelled out clearly, followed by the ordeal in which only his sheer will to live and his physical endurance carry him through the test; and (5) the complete destruction (usually) of the adversary, even though 007 may have to be rescued by a compatriot before his "safe" return. The pattern bears close analogy to the adventures of the mythological hero which Joseph Campbell discusses definitively in *The Hero with a Thousand Faces.* The processes are identical but the metaphors have been changed—a .25 Beretta instead of a sword, a flamethrowing marsh buggy instead of a real live dragon.

Although each of the novels can stand on its own relative merits within the "thriller" genre, collectively the series is more than the sum of its parts. In totality it serves to provide the book which Bond had wished for in Fleming's first novel, *Casino Royale,* in a chapter entitled "The Nature of Evil":

> There's a Good Book about goodness and how to be good and so forth, but there's no Evil Book about evil and how to be bad. The Devil had no prophets to write his Ten Commandments, and no team of authors to write his biography. His case has gone completely by default. We know nothing about him but a lot of fairy stories from our parents and schoolmasters. He has no book from which we can learn the

> nature of evil in all its forms, with parables about evil people, proverbs about evil people, folklore about evil people. (CR, p. 11)[5]

At this early point in his career as a secret service agent, Bond is ready to resign. In fact, he actually has reached the point of considering the whole business of spying as utterly futile, a viewpoint which has been the major premise also in John Le Carré's two best-selling spy novels, *The Spy Who Came in from the Cold* and *The Looking Glass War*. But whereas Le Carré has expanded and deepened this perspective most effectively, Fleming sums it up in the phrase "playing Red Indians" and sends Bond off on a different tack. The takeoff point is delineated clearly in this one chapter in the conversation between Bond and his French counterpart, Mathis, as well as in the other books when Fleming discusses how rapidly national enemies become friends over the course of history.

In this talk, which takes place after Bond has nearly recovered from the torture he suffered under the sadistic hands of the SMERSH agent Le Chiffre, Bond points out to Mathis that when we are young, it is very easy to distinguish between right and wrong, but that as we grow older the process becomes more difficult. He says that at school "it's easy to pick out one's own villains and heroes, and one grows up wanting to be a hero and kill the villains."

However, out in the field, after killing two villains and becoming a Double O number in the Service, he begins to see that the villains and heroes get all mixed up. Even though patriotism can make the process seem all right in the beginning, "this country-right-or-wrong business is getting a little out of date." He points out that, although today we are fighting communism, the brand of conservatism which Britain has today would have been called communism by those who lived fifty years ago, and that he would have been told to go and fight that. "History is moving pretty quickly these days, and the heroes and villains keep on changing parts."

It is only in encountering Le Chiffre (Fleming's fictional version of a French Communist and paymaster of the Soviet murder organization SMERSH) that Bond began to see that this evil man had really served a "wonderful" purpose:

> . . . a really vital purpose, perhaps the best and highest purpose of all. By his evil existence, which foolishly I have helped to destroy, he was creating a norm of badness by which, and by which alone, an opposite norm of goodness could exist. We were privileged, in our short knowledge of him, to see and estimate his wickedness, and we emerge from the acquaintanceship better and more virtuous men. (*Ibid.*)

After a satiric interchange, Mathis agrees with Bond's premise about evil but refuses to accept his resignation:

> . . . now that you have seen a really evil man you will know how evil they can be, and you will go after them to destroy them in order to protect yourself and the people you love. You won't wait or argue about it. You know what they look like now and what they can do to people. You may be a bit more choosy about the jobs you take on. You may want to be certain that the target really is black; but there are plenty of really black targets around. There's still plenty for you to do. . . . Surround yourself with human beings, my dear James. They are easier to fight for than principles. . . . But don't let me down and become human yourself. We would lose such a wonderful machine. (pp. 112-113)

Although Mathis' speech helps to instigate Bond's pursuit of various forms of evil in the subsequent adventures, his final warning is disregarded. Before the end of the first novel Bond is already well on the way in a "humanization" process. Initially, we read, he has never been made to suffer "by cards or by women," knowing that when that happened he too would be branded with the "deadly question-mark" which he had recognized so often in others, "the promise to pay before you have lost; the acceptance of fallibility." In *Casino Royale* both cards and a woman go wrong for him: by the eleventh chapter ("The Moment of Truth") he had been beaten and cleaned out at cards, and it is only because of Felix Leiter's contribution that he is able to continue and win all of Le Chiffre's money; and at the end of the book the integrity of his love for Vesper Lynd disintegrates with her suicide and the realization that she had been a double agent.

The losses which Bond suffers in this book—at cards, in love, and by physical torture (a diabolical "spanking")—set the pattern for each of the following books, in which he gradually becomes less machine-like and more human, until finally he is the bumbling operative whom the critics josh and suggest should be renumbered "006½." At the conclusion of *Casino Royale* Bond realizes that in his previous career he has merely been playing at the child's game of Red Indians, and so he resolves to leave the business of espionage to the "white-collar boys" who can "spy and catch the spies," while he himself will "go after the threat behind the spies, the threat that made them spy."

In the pursuit of Bond's pledge Fleming leads the readers of his subsequent adventures down a Möbius-strip primrose path into a surrealistic world in which things are seldom what they seem to be. Evidences of this verbal surrealism are to be found in Fleming's hyper-attention to minuscule details, his disregard for really probable plots, the poetic "fancies" of the names he gives his characters, and the description of surrealistic scenes in which he comments upon the strange unreality of a particular situation. These verbal characteristics are directly analogous to the visual images which have been presented by such artists as Salvador Dali, Yves Tanguy, Max Ernst, and Peter Blume who took part in the surrealist movement following World War I with a radical questioning of man's rational abilities and value systems.

Although other critics have complained about his plots and compiled lists of what Amis termed the "Fleming effect," the Fleming mystique about names has been relatively ignored. His friends may have shuddered to find their names casually dropped onto a character just for the fun of it; besides friends (Leiter) and associates (Harling), Fleming even christened one of the innocent country girls in *On Her Majesty's Secret Service* with an abbreviated version of his wife's name (Anne Charters). It is not unusual to find the phonetic spelling of a name, rather than its customary usage, e.g., Mr. and Mrs. Phancey in *The Spy Who Loved Me* and even Sean Connery's first name in another very intriguing passage.

The most fun comes, however, when one tallies up the list of characters in an entire novel; in *Diamonds Are Forever* the villains are American members of a "Spangled Mob," the heroine is Tiffany Case, the jockeys are "Tingaling" Bell and Tommy T. Lucky, the various thugs are "Lame-Brain" Pissaro, "Rosy" Budd, "Boofy" Kidd, and "Windy" Wint, all of whom are led by "Shady" Tree. A tally of the entire list of characters soon leads one to believe that Fleming was having a grand time of spoofing someone with them, all in contradiction to the dictate that a "rose is a rose is a rose."

The uncanny aspects of many geographical scenes in the novels directly resemble the surrealist school of painting, e.g., Fleming's description of the rocket-launch site in *Moonraker*:

> It looked like a newly laid aerodrome or rather, he thought, with its three disparate concrete "things", the beehive dome, the flat-iron blast-wall, and the distant cube of the firing point, each casting black pools of shadow towards him in the early sun, like a Dali desert landscape on which three *objets trouvés* reposed at carefully calculated random. (M, p. 89)

Fleming reserves his primary surrealistic effect, however, for secret agent 007's encounters with the grotesque caricatures who serve as the various personifications of evil in the twentieth-century world. We shall take a closer look at each of them in a later chapter, as each of them is a representation of a villain whose appearance is "larger than life." The description of Doctor No contains the most explicit surrealistic reference:

> It was impossible to tell Doctor No's age: as far as Bond could see, there were no lines on the face. It was odd to see a forehead as smooth as the top of the polished skull. Even the cavernous indrawn cheeks below the prominent cheekbones looked as smooth as fine ivory. There was something Dali-esque about the eyebrows, which were fine and black and sharply upswept as if they had been painted on as make-up for a conjurer. . . . The bizarre, gliding figure looked like a giant venomous worm wrapped in grey tinfoil, and Bond would not have been surprised to see the rest of it trailing slimily along the carpet behind. (DN, p. 130)

If Fleming had pitted his secret agent 007 only against the

realistic enemies in the "normal" spy routine, one would not have been able to perceive so clearly his basic intention. In *Goldfinger,* however, he provides his own clue: "Goldfinger said, 'Mr. Bond, they have a saying in Chicago: "Once is happenstance, twice is coincidence, the third time it's enemy action."'" To continue the metaphor, by the time Bond has tilted with his fourth adversary we may be sure that the series is concerned with armed warfare against Satan's contemporary minions.

Fortunately our hypothesis does not have to rest upon the evidence presented in this surrealistic questioning of values in the Bond series alone. For in instigating the original idea for, and publication of, *The Seven Deadly Sins,* Fleming provided left-handed direct evidence for what his right hand had been doing indirectly all along. In this collection of essays by seven distinguished authors on the seven ancient deadly sins (Envy, Pride, Covetousness, Gluttony, Sloth, Lust, Anger), Fleming admits his own "dreadful conclusion that in fact all these ancient sins, compared with the sins of today, are in fact very close to virtues." He sees how each of them could be used strategically to combat greater evils—"as for Anger surely we all need more rather than less of it to combat the indifference, the 'I'm all right, Jack' attitudes, of today." And he suggests that all of those seven ancient virtues likewise possess their own demonic counterpoints today.

The archdemon of Fleming's original roster of sins is the spirit of accidie (or accidia or acedia), which may be translated as indifference, carelessness, or apathy. Bond encounters this spirit not only in the caricatures of "Mr. Big" in *Live and Let Die,* Doctor No, and "Blofeld" alias "Shatterhand," but also in himself as well. As Fleming puts it: "Of all the seven, only Sloth in its extreme form of *accidia,* which is a form of spiritual suicide and a refusal of joy . . . has my wholehearted condemnation, perhaps because in moments of despair I have seen its face."[6]

In addition, even though he recognizes that the great authors could not have written their masterpieces without the depiction of the seven sins and their consequences, Fleming suggests a list of "seven deadlier sins": Avarice, Cruelty, Snobbery, Hypocrisy, Self-Righteousness, Moral Cowardice, and Malice. In doing so he points to his own hypothesis: "If I were to put these modern seven into the scales against the ancient seven I cannot but feel that the weight of the former would bring the brass tray crashing down." More startling yet, he concludes: "As a man in the street, I can only express my belief that being possessed of the ancient seven deadly sins one can still go to heaven, whereas to be afflicted by the modern variations can only be a passport to hell."

In an interview with a *New Yorker* reporter a year before his death, Fleming accounted for Bond's amazing popularity:

> I think the reason for his success is that people are lacking in heroes in real life today. Heroes are always getting knocked—Philip and Mountbatten are examples of this . . . Well, I don't regard James Bond precisely as a hero, but at least he does get on and do his duty, in an extremely corny way, and in the end, after giant despair, he wins the girl or the jackpot or whatever it may be. My books have no social significance, except a deleterious one; they're considered to have too much violence and too much sex. But all history has that.[7]

It is here that our hypothesis can continue to suggest that perhaps Fleming's tacit intent in writing the Bond series was to name and to destroy the modern gods of our society which are actually the expressions of the demonic in contemporary disguise.

While visiting a battlefront during World War II as part of his duty as a commander in the British Naval Intelligence directing the activities of his own Red Indian group, the Number 30 Assault Unit, Fleming announced to a friend that after the war he intended to write the "spy-story to end all spy-stories." In many respects he has fulfilled his prophecy, despite the friend's almost choking on his Spam at the time. Critics have viewed the Bond adventures from various angles: yet one clue which they have overlooked is Fleming's own suggestion that we have been looking for sin in the wrong places, that we must go "after the threat behind the spies, the threat that made them spy" and the source behind the obvious source—not automation or the bomb but man's inhumanity and apathy regarding his fellowman. By adopting the thriller genre despite all its "sex, sadism and snobbery"—bait for public appeal—Fleming has been able to give self-awareness a "sting from behind."

But his cleverness was not restricted to only this sleight-of-hand operation, for by examining the most notorious of the adventures, we can turn the screw one more notch and see the next trick he brought into play against, as well as for, the reader.

003 • Doctor No Revisited

Quarrel:
"People dem want different tings in dis world.
An what dem want sufficient dem gits." (DN, p. 38)

The great critical hoopla about all of the Bond books began to snowball after the publication of *Doctor No,* the sixth book in the series. Although the first five adventures had met with only routine responses from newspaper and magazine critics either attracted or repelled according to personal tastes, *Doctor No* provoked explosive reactions when it was published in 1958. If one counts the actual number of words in reviews listed in the *Book Review Digest,* it is apparent that this was the most notorious of all the books and it seems quite appropriate that it was made into the first movie. Actually Fleming had invited special consideration for *Doctor No,* because it presented the return of James Bond after his apparent death in the conclusion of *From Russia with Love,* a death which early fans in England had rebelled against just as vociferously as Sherlock Holmes devotees once regretted that detective's temporary disappearance.

However, even though the fans were happy to have Bond back, the critics began their great divide—either they loved the books quite irrationally or they hated them just as passionately. A few reviewers were frankly appreciative, e.g., James Sandoe, who termed it the "astutest of elegant leg-pulls . . . the most artfully bold, dizzyingly poised thriller of a decade," and L. G. Offord, who similarly considered it "hair-raising," but also "so wildly funny that it might almost be a leg-pull." *Saturday*

Review was content to call it "an erudite cliff-hanger with sex-sauce," but Anthony Boucher, the true connoisseur of the spy-detective genre, deplored it for being 80,000 words long with plot only enough for 8000 words and originality for 800! Frankly I would reverse his numbers, saying that Fleming had begun with one of the most ancient and familiar of plots consisting of eight words which his originality spun off into 80,000 words in *Doctor No* with various themes and variations extending out into all of the other long and short versions!

Although Robert Hatch had disdained *Doctor No* as a "concentrated example of published nastiness!" the most virulent counterattack was mounted by Paul Johnson in the British publication, the *New Statesman,* under a title which has been misquoted without credit ever since: "Sex, Snobbery and Sadism." Johnson termed it the "nastiest book ever written" and one which he was able to continue reading only because he realized that "here was a social phenomenon of some significance." In his opinion there were only:

> three basic ingredients in *Doctor No,* all unhealthy, all thoroughly English: the sadism of a schoolboy bully, the mechanical, two-dimensional sex longings of a frustrated adolescent, and the crude, snob-cravings of a suburban adult. Mr. Fleming has no literary skill, the construction of the book is chaotic, and entire incidents and situations are inserted, and then forgotten, in a haphazard manner. But the three ingredients are manufactured and blended with deliberate professional precision: Mr. Fleming dishes up his recipe with all the calculated accountancy of a Lyons Corner House.[1]

Needless to say, such critical reaction was better for the sales of the book in Britain than having a book banned in Boston would be in the United States, and one could say that the Bond phenomenon was launched with *Doctor No.* Of course, various other factors which are extraneous to the books themselves have been suggested, such as their great popularity with the British upper class, the appreciation of them in the United States by President Kennedy and Allen Dulles, as well as the frank appeal which they have for adolescent males looking for a continuation of some secret formula regarding cars, liquor, and women (the same appeal which *Playboy* magazine has pyramided into a titanic enterprise).

It is doubtful that Fleming himself as a writer could have resented the critics' malevolent attacks entirely, for apparently these reviews only served to increase his readership on the one hand; and on the other such reaction was proof that his bait had been taken by the fish. However, the misleading emphasis upon "sex, snobbery and sadism" and the false impression of the Bond "style of life" meant that Fleming was forced to counteract the emphasis which was being placed upon the wrong syllable, i.e., upon James Bond whom Fleming had designed originally just as the blunt instrument to perform as the agent in his hidden drama about evil. His attempts to restore a balance with his own perspective appear directly in several adventures. Although *The Spy Who Loved Me* is written in the style of a true-confession type of novelette on a soap-opera level, it presents a devastating parody of the misuse and manipulation of sex. Snobbery is the Achilles' heel which almost defeats Blofeld in *On Her Majesty's Secret Service,* and accordingly presents Fleming with many opportunities to mock those overly concerned about family lineage and coats of arms (cf. SS, p. 86).

One must try to appreciate the particular problem Fleming faced in his chosen genre as he attempted to convince his readers that all *human* life is of value. As a person Fleming himself was a man who could not even bear to have the rats killed at his Jamaican home—to Sir Anthony Eden's discomfiture and hence rapid extermination of the same when he had rented the property. The villains whom Bond was "licensed to kill" were all deliberately described as "larger than life," but still this distinction is difficult to maintain, especially if the reader is not to suspect his ulterior motives. Consequently Fleming was having to repeat constantly that Bond could never kill in cold blood, but only in situations in which he faced being killed himself (or had been brainwashed by an adversary).

The beginning of *Goldfinger,* which followed *Doctor No,* presents one of Fleming's strongest attempts to re-establish his own values: "James Bond, with two double bourbons inside him, sat in the final departure lounge of Miami Airport and thought about life and death." He had just been forced to kill an "evil man" on one of his minor assignments, but he meditates:

> What an extraordinary difference there was between a body full of person and a body that was empty! Now there is someone, now there is no more. This had been a Mexican with a name and an address, an employment card and perhaps a driving licence. Then something had gone out of him, out of the envelope of flesh and cheap clothes, and had left him an empty paper bag waiting for the dust-cart. And the difference, the thing that had gone out of the stinking Mexican bandit, was greater than all Mexico. (pp. 7-8)

It is hard to decide just exactly what metaphor to use when describing Fleming's literary strategy. We could say that he concocted a verbal monkey trap so that his readers were compelled to get more than they reached for originally. Or we might say that he took an old, old recipe for serving a mass audience, spiced it up a bit, and then repackaged it in a new container. As I've suggested in the preceding chapter, there's nothing secret about what he was doing—everything he had to do and say was out in plain sight, just as in Poe's case of the purloined letter.

The situation seems quite akin to that of Søren Kierkegaard, who also wrote material for both direct and indirect communication, but on a much deeper level. It has been said that the one thing which that great Dane feared most of all was that his work might fall into the hands of the professors. From Fleming's own comments one may be quite certain that the last thing which he wanted also was for his *ouvre* to fall prematurely into the hands of either literary or social critics. It seems that he consciously downgraded his work so that whatever didactic element it does contain might remain unstated, and, therefore, by being well-dramatized, be able to insinuate itself through art (as in the plays by Ibsen and Shaw). By maintaining his own "cover" as the mercenary author of thrillers designed merely to attract the mass public, Fleming could be sure that the attention of his audience would not be deflected from the narrative action to the more serious matters which he was insinuating subliminally in the background.

The catch in this whole process is that people have been content to take Fleming's statements at face value, as he had kept insisting that they should, and they believe that his chief goal was limited to what he had said—to get adolescents of all ages to turn the page. This is quite akin to the surrealist painter, René Magritte, who painted a picture of a pipe and lettered underneath "This is not a pipe" or an image of a commonplace tuba which announces it is not a tuba because it has burst into flames. As John Canaday comments, "The constant implication in a painting by Magritte is that nothing unusual is going on, and that only our own dull-wittedness in the experience of daily life has kept us from seeing the nature of Magritte's fantastic world."[2] That Fleming was aware of the same distortions our private perspectives can produce is evident in one of Bond's reflections in the last novel:

> This was always happening in his particular trade. You were looking in the dark for a beetle with red wings. Your eyes were focused for that particular pattern on the bark of the tree. You didn't notice the moth with the cryptic colouring that crouched quietly nearby, itself like a piece of the bark, itself just as important to the collector. The focus of your eyes was too narrow. Your mind was too concentrated. You were using 1 by 100 magnification, and your 1 by 10 was not in focus. (GG, p. 94)

Of course, as Kingsley Amis has said, if you want to be known as a great writer, you don't go around calling your work piffle, which Fleming cheerfully did. On the other hand, Fleming's own reaction to Amis' comment would probably have been a huge laugh and a quiet aside that one can't go around being a great bore either, telling people how significant your works are going to be a few years hence.

Our problem at this point consists of keeping the Bond series within the 1 by 10 focus in order to see just what Fleming was up to. In addition to the most obvious direct communication which Fleming made in *The Seven Deadly Sins* as discussed above, there are a variety of subtle indications which suggest that his "game" was deliberately oblique. There is the magic car GEN-11 in his delightful children's book, *Chitty-Chitty-Bang-Bang,* which only the knowing can recognize as "genii." There is Fleming's constant concern for Bond's cover as well as his search for the "invisible pattern" and the "invisible man." There is also the incongruity between his proud claim, on the one hand, to have learned to write rapidly and accurately while he was a foreign correspondent for Reuters, and, on the other hand, his obvious goofs which he let ride in many books, e.g., Sing-Sing as a women's prison, the wrong kind of brakes on the Orient Express, the mistakes in perfume and guns (all of which stimulated his readers to look more closely at the "Fleming effect"). Tangentially, one might also consider Fleming's own interest in collecting the world's most pivotal books since the eighteenth century, his sponsorship of the most erudite magazine in the world on book collecting, his excellent collection of antique brasses of gods and goddesses, and his reported penchant for rambling about London seeking out old churches.

In addition, in a magazine interview Fleming admitted quite candidly that he thought that his readers enjoyed and accepted his little idiosyncracies and didn't stop to think about them. As he said, "The pace of the narrative gets one by these nasty little corners. It's a sleight of hand operation. It's overpowering the reader. You take him along at such a rate, you interest him so deeply in the narrative that he isn't jolted by these incongruities. I suppose I do it to demonstrate that I *can* do it."[3]

The whole process seems to be a sort of literary "Hidden Persuader" similar to the hypnotic one Fleming devised for the villain Blofeld (alias Bleuville) to use on the simple country girls in *On Her Majesty's Secret Service:*

> Deep hypnosis! That was what he had heard. The Hidden Persuader! The repetitive, singsong message injected into the brain while it was on the twilight edge of consciousness. Now, in Ruby's subconscious, the message would work on all by itself through the night, leaving her, after weeks of repetition, with an in-built mechanism of obedience to the voice that would be as deep, as compelling, as hunger. (p. 104)

We begin to wonder what was the message which Fleming might have been trying to instill. Was it simply a "most harmless, even a praiseworthy message," or, like Blofeld, did Fleming have a more sinister intent? What was the pattern which he planned? We might even ask, "Whose pattern?" as Bond did at the conclusion of *Moonraker,* when Sir Hugo Drax's diabolical plan to blow up London might have succeeded "but for a whole pattern of tiny circumstances, a whole pattern of chance."

Of course, the whole question of whether Fleming really did have a master plan for the entire Bond series is one which his fans and critics may speculate over for years (unless he left some concrete direct evidence, perhaps in a secret file entitled "For Your Eyes Only" or written in homemade invisible ink in his own passport). I prefer to take as my starting point the chapter in *Casino Royale* which points ahead to the development of a portfolio of scenes, a collection of parables, proverbs, and folklore about the devil in the shape of evil people. Perhaps Fleming planned ahead for his little literary "game," his "spy-story to end all spy-stories," just as Bond had planned ahead for his evening's game at the Casino:

> There remained an hour . . . an hour to examine minutely the details of his plans for the game, and for after the game, in all the various circumstances of victory or defeat. He had to plan the attendant roles of Mathis, Leiter, and the girl and visualize the reactions of the enemy in various contingencies. He closed his eyes, and his thoughts pursued his imagination through a series of carefully constructed scenes as if he were watching the tumbling chips of coloured glass in a kaleidoscope. (CR, p. 44)

Actually Fleming has set up the whole pattern very neatly: by introducing each of his major themes in the early novels, then by bringing them into precise relationships and focus in *Doctor No,* and finally by playing around with them in the following adventures, just as one spins the color chips in a kaleidoscope, developing various aspects and permutations. The simple little eight-word plot which Fleming apparently utilized as the basic matrix within which he manipulated all of his plots was just this: "St. George slays evil dragon, rescues forlorn princess." Fleming's use and transformation of this plot reflects his own real genius, for this theme is the ideal vehicle for him to employ as an "objective correlative" in parallel with his questioning the seven deadly sins of the twentieth century. This theme is part of an ancient legend which most people are acquainted with only superficially as a cultural relic or cliché, but it has played an important role in the traditional symbolism of the Christian faith because it represents the continuing encounter between good and evil. First, therefore, let's review this ancient theme, which strikes deeply into what Jung has termed the "collective unconscious" of the human race, and then we'll be able to see how Fleming has recast it in completely contemporary form.

The legend of St. George and the dragon has been retold in a wide variety of ways ever since it was first melded onto the meager historical data concerning the early Christian martyr known as St. George. However, the basic version may be summed up by stating that there was once a small town somewhere along the Mediterranean coast which had been threatened by a dreadful dragon with poisonous breath. In order to guarantee that this evil dragon would not destroy the entire town, the villagers were required to furnish him with two small lambs every day. Since their supply of lambs was soon exhausted, the villagers were forced to resort to drawing lots in order to select which of the town's youth would be sacrificed instead.

This process continued until the day when the name of the town's princess was drawn. With great sorrow the villagers led her out to the swamp where the dragon lived and left her there alone to die. Immediately thereafter, of course, that young nobleman and soldier later known as St. George happened to ride by and came to her rescue.

At this point there are two major variations of the legend. In the first, St. George had become identified with the chivalrous knights of the Crusades and was able to kill the dragon only after a great struggle. This scene of violence, often embellished with the grisly remnants of previous victims as well as the terrified maiden, has been depicted by such great artists as Raphael, Tintoretto, Carpaccio, Uccello, and Delacroix. The second version, which appears in countless church panels and illuminated manuscripts, is more apologetic. In it St. George does not kill the dragon immediately, but instead binds its neck with the princess's sash and leads it into the village. After suitably impressing the townspeople with the necessity of their conversion to Christianity, he then kills the dragon in the village square. Refusing the hand of the princess in marriage, he then distributes his reward among the poor and rides off alone once more.

Thereafter, St. George reputedly continued doing noble deeds all around the known world until the last and greatest of the Roman persecutions of the Christians in A.D. 303, when he hurried back home to protest the edict of intolerance proclaimed by the Emperor Diocletian. Despite his subsequent arrest and the wide variety of dreadful tortures which he miraculously survived, he continued steadfastly to refuse the worship of pagan gods and consequently was beheaded.

Such bravery has captured the imagination and given great inspiration to countless Christians, not only in his own time, as evidenced by the many churches dedicated in his name by the first Christian emperor, Constantine, but also down through the ages. St. George became the patron saint of many coastal towns, and of soldiers and sailors. More especially he became known as one of the seven great champions of Christendom and the patron saint of England. The red cross of St. George emblazoned upon a field of white was often carried as a banner or worn as an emblem during the Crusades and it is still preserved as the central cross in Great Britain's flag.

Undoubtedly only an Englishman could appreciate most vividly the importance of the image of St. George as a dynamic force within the history of his country. Men like Wordsworth, Ruskin, and John Masefield are among those who have expressed their appreciation for this image and mourned the times when it was dormant. In earlier times St. George held a very special place within the hearts of the people. St. George's day (April 23) was once reverenced as highly as Christmas. Although King Henry VIII was able to abolish all of the other nonbiblical and non-apostolic saints' days from the calendar of the Christian church, St. George's day remained as a day comparable to St. Patrick's day for the Irish. (And King Henry VIII was the king to finish the St. George's Chapel at Windsor Castle!)

Shakespeare's historical plays abound with vivid dramatic evidence of how the image of St. George permeated the life of the English. There are countless examples of the stirring call to battle: "Then strike up drums:—God and Saint George for us!"[4] which is expanded in King Richard the Third's climactic appeal:

> A thousand hearts are great within my bosom:
> Advance our standards, set upon our foes;
> Our ancient word of courage, fair Saint George,
> Inspire us with the spleen of fiery dragons!
> Upon them! Victory sits on our helms.[5]

There is also the long speech of challenge by King Henry the Fifth which begins, "Once more unto the breach, dear friends, once more:" and concludes:

> . . . The game's afoot!
> Follow your spirit, and upon this charge
> Cry "God for Harry, England, and Saint George!"[6]

In addition there is evidence of the high honor in which the Knights of the Garter were held (the order which was established in 1350 by Edward III in honor of St. George and the highest British recognition which is still being given today) as indicated by Talbot's speech in the *First Part of King Henry the Sixth*:

> When first this order was ordain'd my lords,
> Knights of the Garter were of noble birth,
> Valiant and virtuous, full of haughty courage,
> Such as were grown to credit by the wars;
> Not fearing death nor shrinking for distress,
> But always resolute in most extremes.[7]

As Christina Hole points out, the symbol of St. George represents "an enduring symbol of high courage, loyalty, and self-devotion to the cause of the weak and endangered."[8] Although Fleming has represented this image within the métier of the secret agent, he is merely following the precedents of the visual artists, who continually have represented the traditional image within contemporary milieu, and of Edmund Spenser, whose knight in Book I of the *Faerie Queene* is not revealed as St. George until the end of his adventures. Tracing the elements of this legend in the Bond adventures can become a fascinating hobby. Strange as it may seem, the legend is revealed most clearly in *Doctor No,* which may be paraphrased as follows:

Once upon a time on a small cold island there was a man carrying great responsibility who became deeply concerned because two of his countrymen had disappeared without warning on a small warm island far away. He therefore called to him a very brave man, who had just recovered from a miraculous brush with death, and sent him out on a mission to find out what had happened. The brave man soon found out that other men were being destroyed two by two, and he encountered a lovely maiden who told him about an evil dragon which she had even seen quite clearly one night when the moon was full:

> It had two great glaring eyes and a long snout. It had sort of short wings and a pointed tail. It was all black and gold. . . . It went by me. It was making a sort of roaring noise. It went over the marsh and came to some thick mangrove and it simply climbed over the bushes and went on. A whole flock of birds got up in front of it and suddenly a lot of fire came out of its mouth and it burned a lot of them up and all the trees they'd been roosting in. It was horrible. The most horrible thing I've ever seen. (DN, p. 74)

But, even though they were sitting near a swamp from which all manner of curious beasts could emerge, the brave young man apparently would not believe the maiden:

> ". . . I can see you don't believe me," she said in a furious, tense voice. "You're one of these city people. You don't believe anything. Ugh," she shuddered with dislike of him.

He in turn tried to answer her reasonably:

> "Honey, there just aren't such things as dragons in the world. You saw something that looked very like a dragon. I'm just wondering what it was."

She replied very angrily:

> "How do you know there aren't such things as dragons?

> . . . Nobody lives on this end of the island. One could easily have survived here. Anyway, what do you think you know about animals and things?"

She then continued with a list of all the demonic actions that go on between animals, asking him if he'd ever seen any of them happen, like seeing a praying mantis eat her husband after they'd made love, or a scorpion get sunstroke and kill itself with its own sting. Since he hadn't, she dismissed him just like all of the other "city people," and he attempted a feeble reply:

> "Honey, now look here. You know these things. I can't help it that I live in towns. I'd like to know about your things too. I just haven't had that sort of life. I know other things instead. Like . . ." (p. 75)

But after searching his mind, he couldn't think of anything as interesting as hers, and so the brave young man switched her attention to the evil Chinaman whom he suspected would try to kill them. The next day, by the swamp on the island, the dragon actually did appear, killing the brave young man's faithful companion and then taking the hero and the girl captive.

The old myth disappears at that point because the "dragon" turns out to be the black and gold painted marsh buggy sent out by Doctor No which has been equipped with a flamethrower and looks like a "float waiting for the Lord Mayor's Show." But the simple story has done its trick, and by the strange alchemy of the unconscious we are linked up with one of the most potent legends in all history, the legend of St. George and the dragon. James Bond then assumes his other identity, secret agent 007 then becomes the seventh great champion in all Christendom, and Fleming performs the greatest sleight-of-hand operation in literature since the Middle Ages when the original St. George theme was linked with the bravery and courage of the Christian knights on the Crusades, both in legend and in art.

In addition to being rather pedantic and boring, tracing Fleming's pattern through the entire Bond series right now would only spoil the readers' fun. There are a few blatant examples, of course, which no one will fail to miss, such as Bond's rather tired response in *Goldfinger*:

> Bond sighed wearily. Once more into the breach, dear friends! This time it really was St George and the dragon. And St George had better get a move on and do something before the dragon hatched the little dragon's egg he was now nesting so confidently. Bond smiled tautly. Do what? What in God's name was there he could do? (p. 155)

There is also the moment in *On Her Majesty's Secret Service* when a low, white two-seater driven by a girl with a shocking-pink scarf tied around her hair passes Bond as he is driving along dictating in his mind a letter of resignation to "M." This is too much for his split personality for:

> If there was one thing that set James Bond really moving in life, with the exception of gun-play, it was being passed at speed by a pretty girl. . . . The shock of the windhorn's scream had automatically cut out "George," emptied Bond's head of all other thought and brought his car back under manual control. (p. 17)

That same evening in the casino after Bond has redeemed the girl's *coup du déshonneur* at the gambling casino, he reflects:

> . . . he had taken a dislike to the monster from Lille. It would be amusing to reverse the old fable—first to rescue the girl, then to slay the monster. (p. 27)

In general, however, most of the time Fleming disguises the traditional material so that it can be picked up only obliquely. The "dragons" are usually disguised—in *Moonraker* Sir Hugo Drax is the alias which Graf Hugo von der Drache, the unrepentant Nazi, is using (*Drache* is German for dragon), and in *You Only Live Twice* the "dragon" motif is initiated when Tiger Tanaka orders Bond "to enter this Castle of Death and slay the dragon within" (p. 66). When he attempts to do so, he finds Blofeld again, this time disguised under the alias of "Shatterhand" wearing a kimono:

> The square-cut, heavily draped kimono, designed to give the illusion of bulk to a race of smallish men, made something huge out of the towering figure, and the golden dragon embroidery, so easily to be derided as a childish fantasy, crawled menacingly across the black silk and seemed to spit real fire from over the left breast. (p. 145)

Similarly, the princess from Trebizond (one of the locations for her home) never appears precisely, although in *From Russia with Love* Tatiana Romanova is a distant relative of the overthrown Russian dynasty and Darko Kerim is a man from Trebizond. In addition, the girl named Ruby in *On Her Majesty's Secret Service* happens to be the daughter of George Albert Windsor and is described as standing there "like a great lovely doll, passive, slightly calculating, wanting to be a princess" (p. 97).

Although many things about James Bond have been "shocking" (especially in the movie *Goldfinger*), it will probably prove more re-volting for many people on both sides of the prudent curtain to accept this connection between secret agent 007 and the legendary figure of St. George. Somehow it's easier to believe that a supposedly good man can have an evil alter ego, such as the dual personality of Dr. Jekyll and Mr. Hyde, than to imagine that a devilish fellow like James Bond could possess the *altar* ego that St. George used to be. But once this incredible proposition begins to sink in, one can appreciate a little better the humor of Ian Fleming's self-styled epitaph, "Oh, it's all been a tremendous lark!"

There are two final bits of evidence which should help to convince even the most skeptical readers. The first is a direct quote from Fleming himself which he gave in an interview shortly before his death: " 'I've got the usual vices myself—Selfishness, and so on,' Fleming confessed, 'But Bond is really a latter-day St. George. He does kill wicked dragons after all.' "[9] The second, which reinforces this statement, is a short sentence from *On Her Majesty's Secret Service*:

> "In my profession," said Bond prosily, "the exact meaning of words is vital." (p. 76)

After appreciating something of the total meaning of the image of St. George conquering the dragon, which is more important as a whole image than the sum of its parts, it is necessary to break it apart into its various elements to see how they relate to our syncopated society. In the next chapter we shall investigate the implications of the image of the secret agent as a modern St. George, and in subsequent chapters we shall take a closer look at the major dragons threatening us.

004 • The Hot Image in the Cold World

> It is as if, beneath the words of contemporary speech and in the images that crowd in upon his imagination, the poet could sense the ghostly presence of bygone spiritual worlds and possessed the capacity to make them come alive again.[1]
>
> C. G. Jung

By one of the weird coincidences created by the strange alchemy of modern business practices within the motion picture industry, the fourth movie in the Bond saga, *Thunderball,* opened in New York metropolitan area theatres on December 21, 1965. The date in itself was not important, but the fact that it marked the night of the winter solstice is intriguing.

The shivering fans, who were willing to tear themselves away from preparations for Hanukkah and Christmas in order to wait in line that night, probably couldn't have cared less, except that the night was particularly cold and the wind biting. The producers of the film undoubtedly were only trying to beat the Academy Award deadlines, perhaps competing for the special effects trophy against *Goldfinger* which had been released earlier in the year.

Yet, if we consider that the James Bond phenomenon derives much of its power from a genuine need for a contemporary hero figure to slay contemporary dragons, then the coincidence is uncanny. Suddenly this latest mass-media symbol had zeroed in on the night on which in ancient times the first storytellers were compelled by the terrors of primitive man to form images of hero figures who could rescue the day from the terrors of the long winter night! The figure of Bond consequently joins a long rank of mythological and literary figures who have served as symbols of transformation at various times of cultural crisis in the Western world.

Within secular writings, such a list of heroes would include the figures of Perseus, Hercules, Hiawatha, Beowulf, Rustam of Persia, and Christian of *Pilgrim's Progress,* to name only a few. Within the Old Testament and Apocrypha there are the stories of David fighting Goliath and Daniel conniving against Bel and the dragon. In the New Testament the book of Mark is full of the stories of Jesus casting out demons, and the book of Luke presents the story of the temptation by the devil in the wilderness. The allegorical book of Revelation contains the figure of the archangel Saint Michael fighting against the dragon—that ancient serpent, who is the devil and Satan. Within the Christian faith it is important to note briefly at this point that the earliest understanding of the atonement presented the dramatic, mythological account of Christ's work as a victory over the devil: Christ is seen as *Christus Victor* fighting against and triumphing over the evil powers of the world, the "tyrants" under which mankind is in bondage and suffering.

The appearance and public acceptance of the fantastic mythological elements of the Bond phenomenon at this time is of particular interest, therefore, for we are at a time in history when, as Buber has pointed out, "the image-making power of the human heart has been in decline so that the spiritual pupil can no longer catch a glimpse of the appearance of the Absolute."[2]

The condition of the times is reminiscent of the scene in the movie *Goldfinger* in which James Bond is left alone temporarily in the depths of Fort Knox. His opponents are that monstrous human parody, Oddjob, and a neatly packaged atom bomb which has a timing mechanism moving down to zero. Can Bond manage to overcome these two dragons of dehumanization and automation? Yes, but only after a manner of speaking. He does manage to execute Oddjob and to break open the locked cover of the bombcase, only to be confronted by an amazing array of spinning dials with variegated wires leading in and out of various mechanisms. Then, as his hand reaches hesitantly first to one unlikely spot and then another, the countdown edges closer to the moment of detonation—112 . . . 111 . . . 110. . . .

However, before Bond's bumbling hands actually can do anything, another hand competently reaches down over his shoulder and flips off a simple switch. Help had arrived just in time—help which he had contrived the evening before by his appeal to Pussy Galore's "maternal instincts." With a deft touch of humor, the spinning dial stops exactly at 007!

Whatever elements may have been left out of Fleming's original formula by scriptwriter Richard Maibaum and the special effects teams when they responded to public interest in adapting the Bond series for the movies, at this point they took the whole saga one step further. Somehow the entire scene sums up the fantastic gift of the storyteller who can build tension in the members of his audience to a climactic breaking point and then release it in one delightful moment of catharsis. But, even more significantly, the appearance of the Bond phenomenon at this particular moment of countdown in history suggests that the power of the creative artist to evolve images and symbols of transformation has not been lost.

Although the introduction of the image of the secret agent is accordingly of great significance at this time, before examining it in detail, it will be helpful to review briefly the concept of images in general. We are in a time when people in many fields have become vitally concerned with images. Images can inform and educate, they can relate or corrupt relationships, they can form illusions or they can disillusion. Many corporations and famous individuals have hired public relations experts in order to improve their public images. Much of our foreign policy has been involved in attempting to maintain a particular image of our country overseas. Even the United States Navy has admitted that its image needs refurbishing, and there is at least one private firm in New York City which advertises that it can help private individuals do the same.

Because a great deal of this activity is concerned with increasing the illusions of the public about what is really happening or about what is really real, instead of actually reporting the news or improving a product or a person, Daniel J. Boorstin has written a guide to the pseudo-events in America today in his book *The Image*. From a slightly different perspective, economist Kenneth Boulding believes that all of our behavior depends upon the images we hold and suggests that the image lies behind the actions of every individual and accounts for the growth of every cause. By understanding the image behind the individual or the cause, we can begin to understand what gives each vitality and meaning. In his book, also entitled *The Image,* he proposes an entirely new interdisciplinary field for the study of images which might be called "eiconics."[3]

Actually images have been of interest to art authorities for a long time in the field known as iconology, which (in art) is the analysis of various elements within art objects, and a science of "eiconics" might benefit greatly from such studies as Edwin Panofsky's breakdown of the elements of iconographical description, analysis, and interpretation. From art experts such as Herbert Read and Suzanne K. Langer and from psychoanalysts from Jung to Daniel E. Schneider, we can learn how the creative artist is able to *re-present* reality for the expansion of man's conscious knowledge about himself. As Read points out in *Icon and Idea*:

> It is only in so far as the artist establishes symbols for the representation of reality that mind, as structure of thought, can take shape. The artist establishes these symbols by becoming conscious of new aspects of reality, and by representing his consciousness of these new aspects of reality in plastic or poetic images.[4]

Because of these creative representations of current reality, the artist is able to help close the gap which results from the lag between man's tool-making and myth-making processes and to help reduce the tension in a syncopated society. The image serves as the "symbol of transformation" by which past is knit to present in order to provide a meaningful pattern of existence which is valid for a particular point in history, never an absolute truth valid for eternity. As a part of the myth-making process an image should be considered along with myth, which can be viewed not so much as an intellectual precipitate of a society as "an idiom in which given groups may communicate to each other both their unity and their disagreements (E. R. Leach)."[5]

Images are essential, therefore, for the communication between individuals which makes possible a positive sense of community. For, as Read states:

> We establish love by communication, and over against the unconscious group soul, we must create a conscious group soul, a community of integrated and interrelated personalities. The means towards this end are always active.[6]

It is in this context, then, that we may review the various attributes of the image of the secret agent. The appeal of this image is immediate, linking cold-war tension of the present with the archetypal qualities of the hero figure of classical mythology, and representing the past in the idiom of the present, not under the banner of great literature but rather through the penetrating gift of the popular storyteller to capture the spirit of the times.

As a symbol of transformation in the mass media, the image of the secret agent is peculiarly resonant with both John MacMurray's philosophical presentation of the "self as agent" and Dietrich Bonhoeffer's concept of the Christian as the responsible agent or deputy (cf. his *Ethics*). It is important to note therefore that the adventures of the secret agent present a radical shift from the previous pattern of detective stories in which someone with a problem could go to some cerebral figure in an armchair for a pat solution to all of his difficulties. The hero or protagonist now is the man with the problem or assignment himself, and it is in acting within a situation that his mission is accomplished. There is no set answer which can be predicted rationally ahead of time. Instead, the agent must be prepared to cope with any contingency, to handle any emergency, and to think on his feet. The reader is therefore involved in the reality of acting in the present rather than cogitating over what has happened in the past. By devising the image of the secret agent, contemporary storytellers therefore have responded not only to the real need for a hero figure who can cope uniquely with contemporary insecurities or dragons, but they also have grounded it in the social reality of the times.

Actually the tension which Fleming and all the other writers of the stories about spies and secret agents have been able to exploit is a ready-made one which they can market easily in our syncopated society. It consists of several fuses to which they had only to set a match: first, public curiosity regarding the secret miniature war which apparently is being fought by secret agents in obscure places all around the world; second, the insecurity resulting from the contemporary search for identity in our highly technological urban society; third, the lag which we have seen resulting from man's tool-making (instrumental) capacities advancing faster than his myth-making skills (institutional processes).

Regardless of the accuracy, newspaper headlines in the last twenty years have served only to pique public curiosity regarding the shrouded exploits of such actual secret agents and spies as Abel and Pentovskiy. The Powers' U-2 affair was just one of a series of events which revealed the extraordinary extent to which information and activities secret to most people are shaping the destiny of the world. On the national level alone, such books as Vance Packard's *The Naked Society* only serve to compound this type of insecurity, for they provide evidence not only of the mounting surveillance of private individuals due to the great increase in organized living, but also the garrison state mentality, which, coupled with the pressures resulting from our abundant society, has made investigation into a successful private industry with countless "electronic eyes, ears and memories."

Internationally, it seems quite possible to believe, as J. Bernard Hutton has stated, that perhaps "one man's treachery, one spy's success, could defeat half a world." Arthur Tietjen has said that "security in an international context is a stranger to the free world," and the multitudinous spy novels, movies, and television programs only serve as primers in this type of cold war. Undoubtedly a great deal of the success of all the literature of violence and pursuit stems from the fact that (in Raymond Chandler's words) ours is "not a very fragrant world." British writer Norman Shrapnel has suggested that the main advantage all the writers in this genre have had is "surely the appalling relevance of their subject matter to the real life myth and fantasy of the day."

The unbelievably complex and tangled scheme of action within the sphere of espionage and counter-espionage has been revealed (with some accuracy one hopes) in more than ten books regarding spy operations which were published in the first half of the 1960's alone. Similarly, with the acceptance of the fact that spies and secret agents are on the frontline defense of every nation, public interest has created an entirely new fiction market, with more than seventy spy-adventure novels and their variations published in 1965 alone. As Eric Ambler has pointed out, even though the spy probably has been a member of the second oldest profession in all history, it is only in recent times that the public would accept the fact that such a traditionally despicable character could be of importance to the international affairs of one's own country.

The very real yet mysterious world of the spies has become an object of concern for the average citizen who suddenly realizes that his own night's sleep might depend upon the activities or information gathered by some secret agent halfway around the world. As Shrapnel states, the stories of "all the agents, dupes and chorus of the frustrated ballet of violence in our time are challenged in preposterousness by one thing only—the news in the daily paper."[7]

However, although the successes of the agents go unheralded while their failures are trumpeted (as Kennedy observed regarding the role of the CIA in the Bay of Pigs affair), one suspects that even the news in the papers may not be trusted. For even Arthur M. Schlesinger, Jr., has stated (when apologizing for the misinformation he had relayed as part of the cover story of that debacle), he could never "take the testimony of journalism in such matters seriously again," for their "relation to reality is often less than the shadows in Plato's cave."[8] Consequently, the public can only hope that some of the "fiction" written by those familiar with actual espionage may parallel reality more closely than the "facts" which have been printed publicly. Either way, we would agree with Conrad Knickerbocker, who suggests that the key to the great popularity of the spies rests in the "yearnings of their readers. Baffled by Vietnam, angered by sonic booms, they feel increasingly overwhelmed by the vast forces that now shape events."[9]

This intense interest in spies is paralleled by an equally strong public desire to believe that the secret agent is actually just as friendly and helpful as the old-fashioned grocer down on the corner. It would be delightful to suppose that somewhere in the obscure mists of overseas security operations, there could be hosts of secret agents possessing not only James Bond's derring-do but also the charm and finesse of Scott and Robinson from the television program *I Spy,* or the tongue-in-cheek attitudes of the men from U.N.C.L.E., or Secret Agent John Drake's understated competence, or even Maxwell Smart's fortuitous flukes.

However, despite the delightful addictive quality of these television versions of the spy game which attempt to reduce the tensions of the cold war to a more human scale, another perspective of that game has been presented in the thrillers written by John Le Carré, Len Deighton, and Adam Hall. In their hands the secret agent is revealed as just another dirty pawn on the chessboard of international politics, and espionage becomes just another form of the "organization game." With these versions we suspect that the "real" spy game is probably just as Knickerbocker suggests: a "technological super-system in which the individual operator, although still occasionally useful, is dwarfed by the corporate efficiencies of machines and organizations. The real-life heroes are not the cloak-and-dagger swingers but the anonymous brethren of Francis Gary Powers."

At this point the fictional image of the secret agent as some sort of superhero begins to shrink into a reasonable facsimile of the anonymous man-in-the-street, differing only perhaps in the extent of double dealings into which he may be manipulated as part of the organization game. It is here that we may begin to see a relationship between the image of the secret agent and the identity problem of the individual in mass society. The glamorous adventures of the secret agent are only a fictional cover for the peculiar form of existence which the technological age has forced not only upon the agents but also upon the average individual as well. To understand this relationship, however, we will have to take a closer look at both the image of the secret agent and the whole question of identity formation today.

In attempting to analyze the general image of the secret agent, it is important to remember that we can only indicate what appears to be a trend at the present time. One hundred years from now social historians and anthropologists may be able to trace the development of modern hero figures more accurately, just as Paul Radin has studied the evolution of the hero myth in the culture of the Winnebago Indians.[10] Superficially we might suggest that there is already preliminary evidence to suggest a parallel progression—from the early Trickster stage which began right after World War II with Eric Ambler's "third man theme," into the 1960's in which all three subsequent states appeared almost simultaneously; the Hare which is an immature childlike figure (Maxwell Smart, Henry Phyfe); Red Horn, a more mature solitary hero with superman tendencies (James Bond, John Drake); and the Twins, one extrovert and one introvert (Solo and Kuryakin; Robinson and Scott).

However, in spite of the enormous variation in detail between these contemporary secret agent figures, there are several general characteristics which underlie the appearance of any one of them. When these characteristics are combined they form a particular configuration, a "gestalt" or an image which is actually unique to our time and to this genre. Various authors run permutations upon this image whenever they build a story, either consciously or not, and it is possible for us to examine it as a complete entity in itself.

Perhaps the clearest, briefest, and least artistic summary of the total image of the secret agent has been offered by the words of the song which was used to introduce the television program *Secret Agent*:

There's a man who leads a life of danger,
To everyone he meets, he stays a stranger,
With every move he makes,
Another chance he takes,
Odds are he won't live to see tomorrow.
Secret agent man, secret agent man:
They've given you a number—
And taken 'way your name![11]

Although this may not be a ballad which might be treasured down through the ages, it does suggest many of the major elements of the secret agent image—his anonymity, his solitariness, his precarious way of living. Moving out from it, we can then begin to examine more general characteristics.

Initially we might note that the secret agent is a man who has been given a mission or an assignment of some kind, who is acting all alone or at most with only one or two compatriots, his "fellow professionals." Whatever he is doing, he has been given a certain amount of responsibility and discretion commensurate with his skill and background, but he is aware that his actions and the little bit of information he gains are only a small part of a greater whole. For tension, of course, he has been assigned to a particular hot spot or a suspicious area, and generally it turns out that the fate of the entire free world rests upon his shoulders at that point.

To continue, the next aspect we might observe is that he is usually required to play a role, maintain a cover, and be trained to the extent that his normal instinctive reactions are disciplined so that his pseudo-identity may not be imperiled. As such, we see that the expectation he is playing upon is that his "social identity" will be able to camouflage his real or "total identity"—that observers will not suspect his private mission. The enemy must not suspect who he really is or that he is really just acting out a role for the benefit of his audience. In this process, his "public self" is sharply split from his "private self"—but he is highly cognizant of the difference. In Erving Goffman's terms, the secret agent's ability to maintain "role distance" would be a manifestation of greater maturity; in Peter Berger's categories, the secret agent is able to manipulate the strings of the social fictions in which we are all engaged.[12] Only rarely is the agent so involved in his "pseudo-identity" that he "lives" his role in private as well as public. In fact, the character Leamas in *The Spy Who Came in from the Cold* is one of the very few who "compelled himself to live with the personality he had assumed" and only rarely allowed "himself the dangerous luxury of admitting the great lie he lived."[13]

In the area of the relationships which the agent maintains with other people, we might note next that all of his associations are transient as part of the requirement of his mission. He cannot afford the luxury of projecting any of his own attitudes or presuppositions onto another person; instead he must be shrewdly aware of the other, not only on an intellectual basis, but also on a perceptual or feeling level. At the same time he is skillfully trying to maintain his own cover in order to protect his "private self" and mission, he is also attempting to penetrate any false or pseudo-identity of those around him. This is, in fact, a "reality-centered" operation, as long as the agent is able to perceive persons as they really are, and it is healthy from that standpoint. It is only destructive if this perception is used to manipulate and destroy the innocent.

Of course, one of the chief points which the general public would include in the image of the secret agent is his highly transient relationship with girls. As long as the emphasis is placed upon promiscuity, this is an extremely negative point. Truthfully, however, the association of sex without love in the image of the agent is probably just as far from reality as was the old image in the Middle Ages of the chivalrous knight romantically in love without sex. Neither is probably true except in fantasy, but the hopeful sign is the disappearance of the neurotic equation between sex and an idealized concept of "romantic love." Sociologists Snell and Gail Putney have noted in *Normal Neurosis* that the source of many marital problems stems directly from just such immature concepts of romantic love in marriage. If the image of the agent can dispel the myth of this immature ideal, perhaps it may make a positive contribution to fidelity and genuine intimacy within marriage.

The agent cannot afford the luxury of sentimentality toward

personal belongings and possessions either. He is forced to "use" things, instead of loving them. His only permanent personal possession is his favorite weapon, and it is a traumatic occasion if the spy-boss orders a change. The agent is generally supplied with all the necessary gadgets he might need for his particular assignment, but the fewer things he takes with him the better. His best weapon is his own body, and so he is also "armed" with the knowledge of judo and karate. Because nothing can be left around as a clue to his real identity, all of his clothes, possessions, and even style of living become part of his role or cover, completely impersonal attributes as thoroughly transient as the rest of his life.

In addition, one expects that the agent is loyal to his country and to a vague concept of mankind in general, despite a very low salary and lack of any private personal world of his own, except when at home on leave. In short, he has been forced to know himself as an individual well enough so that he can maintain his value system regardless of any routine situation and particularly in the event of any physical or mental torture. Accordingly, he is required to be a man possessing high mobility, able to cope with rapid changes and to take whatever action may be necessary. He is therefore assumed to be highly responsible and autonomous even in situations of great stress, crisis, and temptation. Thoroughly pragmatic and profane, he is an A-1 candidate for the world of the "secular city" which has been described recently by Harvey Cox. And, if you review the last few paragraphs, you'll observe that most of these characteristics would be quite typical of the mobile, transient upper-management man of the 1960's. Our question is not whether this is already present reality or not, but rather just which aspects we might hope to prevent in the future and which are inevitable. The split has occurred already between one's "public" and "private" identities; the planned obsolescence of the production line already ensures a high turnover of one's possessions; and geographic and economic mobility already disrupt relationships with one's family and friends. It may be that only individual intimacy and commitment will be left in the future.

After considering these initial aspects of the image of the secret agent and their possible relevance to contemporary life, the next major element which should be reviewed is that of the agent's "life of danger" and the crisis situations which he must face. Just as in the typical cowboy tradition and all other genre concerned with good guys versus bad guys, the agent must encounter the enemy and engage in a subsequent fight to the finish. The new element in the pattern of the secret agent genre, however, is a certain type of scene which occurs almost without fail: the "blackout" scene, which may even be found as a separate chapter heading in some books. This scene generally consists of a brutal attack which results in the agent's complete loss of consciousness, followed by a gradual return to his senses, involving his perception of space, time, and identity. Although the situation of encounter may vary from author to author and from book to book, it is a stock item in most plots. It can occur because of torture, as in Fleming:

> Bond wrestled with his consciousness. He screwed up his eyes and tried to shake his head to clear it; but his whole nervous system was numbed, and no message was transmitted to his muscles. He could just keep his focus on the great pale face in front of him and on its bulging eyes. . . . The pain was nothing to what Bond was already suffering, but it was enough to plunge him again into unconsciousness. (CR, pp. 99-101)

or in an unexpected attack, as against Leamas in *The Spy* . . . :

> His hands were still at his side as the blow came. It seemed to crush his skull. As he fell, drifting warmly into unconsciousness, he wondered whether he had been hit with a revolver, the old kind with a swivel on the butt where you fastened the lanyard.[14]

and against Donald Hamilton's Matt Helm:

> . . . I didn't see the dark-faced man move—I wasn't looking that way—but I heard him. There was no point in dodging. Where could I go? I just hoped he was good at his work, and he was. The blow put me out instantly, with hardly any pain at all.[15]

However, the most interesting and unique development of this particular detail of "blackout" is the one employed by Adam Hall in *The Quiller Memorandum,* which I read long after I had formulated my idea about the syncopated society. In this book (in one of the tautest scenes in the genre) the "blackout" is administered initially by hypodermic injections, but a second "blackout" is described later which is achieved by Quiller's deliberate induction in himself of the phenomenon of "syncope."

> She made another sound and I did the one thing that held out any hope.
>
> I fainted.
>
> The last conscious memory was of Oktober reaching out to save my hitting the floor. It was probably instinctive. I was able, before blacking out, to note that he must be ignorant of the processes of syncope, or he wouldn't try to keep me upright. The longer I remained upright, the longer I would remain blacked out.[16]

The significance of these scenes of "blackout," however, is not the means of induction, from torture, attack, or voluntary submission, but rather the event itself, which is directly analogous to the scene of death and rebirth, the loss of the "world-taken-for-granted," the rite of transition, whether you prefer to think of it in psychological, theological, or anthropological terminology. They are the proof text for the new strength of the hero figure who is able to pass through "death" into a new "life"—that he need not face the condemnation which one character stood under in a Matt Helm adventure: "He did not have the courage to die in a situation that required his death."[17]

The recovery from these "blackouts" presents the occasion, therefore, for "rebirth" with the recovery of consciousness and a reorientation to the world:

In Fleming:

> You are about to awaken when you dream that you are dreaming.
>
> During the next two days James Bond was permanently in this state without regaining consciousness. He watched the procession of his dreams go by without making any effort to disturb their sequence, although many of them were terrifying and all were painful. He knew that he was in a bed

> and that he was lying on his back and could not move and in one of his twilight moments he thought there were people round him; but he made no effort to open his eyes and re-enter the world. (CR, pp. 101-102)

and Le Carré:

> He was wakened by the lag singing and the warder yelling at him to shut up. He opened his eyes and like a brilliant light the pain burst upon his brain. He lay quite still, refusing to close them, watching the sharp, colored fragments racing across his vision. He tried to take stock of himself. . . .[18]

Hamilton:

> "Tell them to find the woman," an oddly accented, liquid-sounding female voice was saying, somewhere outside the circle of darkness in which I seemed to lie. . . . I was aware that I was lying in the sun, probably in the spot where I'd fallen, and that a rock was gouging my thigh and an insect crawling up my neck, but everything seemed very pleasant and peaceful. I wasn't really playing possum. I had no urge whatever to open my eyes. I was happy just to lie there and listen.[19]

Hall:

> Voices again. Inga called something. Water running somewhere. A flash of light as Oktober brought the back of his hand across my face. I was moaning. The shock of the water as they flung it against my eyes. Full consciousness came back and I had to feign continuance of the syncope, letting my dead weight hang on their hands as they tried to wake me, letting my lids droop and the eyes turn upward.[20]

By establishing these particular scenes as one phase of the crisis situation of the typical thriller, my concern has not been over their literary merits, but rather their implications as part of the image of the secret agent in relation to the identity crisis of modern man. On an individual level we can presume that the blackout scenes, either verbally as quoted above or visually in the movies and television by swirling images and blurring of focus, present an occasion for a contemporary rite of transition parallel to the puberty rites of primitive man. But on a broader, social level, we might consider a wide implication. For, in the convergence of many factors, blind forces, and disillusionments in the process of social syncopation, just as the secret agent suffers this period of "blackout" or "syncope," the image of contemporary man has been presented with a profound "culture shock" as well.

There is a wide variety of cultural instruments which may be blamed for this form of cultural shock. Someone such as William Barrett would blame the Reformation for stripping the ordinary man of all the comforts, images, and dependency afforded by the Catholic Church. On the other hand, Freud believed that three insults had been presented against man's ego: the cosmic insult of the Copernican revolution, the biological insult presented by Darwin, and his own psychological insult attacking man's rationality. In addition, there is also the cultural insult predicted by such social critics as Marx, Tönnies, Durkheim, Simmel, and Weber, who have depicted man as determined by economic and societal factors, or the assault by the technology of modern industry which Michael Harrington suggests has forced a completely accidental revolution upon mankind. However, it may be that Western civilization is experiencing a delayed shock wave from the real impact of the Christian gospel—now hitting with direct intensity with the disappearance of the Greek metaphysical thought-systems and the removal of the cocoon of Christendom which Søren Kierkegaard insisted had deluded the world into thinking that all are Christians as a matter of course and that the world (or Christendom) could be Christianized. As he said, "The fundamental misfortune of Christianity is Christendom."[21]

But whatever way one might wish to describe the particular insult afforded man's ego, the fact remains that sometime in the last twenty years our particular civilization passed a certain point of no return. The factors precipitating this transition point, which were first recognized aesthetically on the intuitive level by the creative artists within the last century, are now recognized cognitively on a multidisciplinary level in the universities and even more viscerally by the average man, for they hit him where he lives. On a wide cultural basis we've been knocked out, just like the secret agent or Rip Van Winkle, and are just beginning to regain consciousness in a world which has changed overnight. The agent's "blackout" is the analogue for our "culture shock" or "syncope" and there's no turning back. This is not necessarily an evil, for with all of our illusions knocked out of us, perhaps our choices may be clarified. As Ernest Becker states:

> To be unconscious of the crucial factors in the situation to which one is adjusting, is to repeat as an adult the early slavery of the child. It is to consent to have one's choices constricted by the accidents of being thrown into a certain kind of world, a world beyond one's powers, beyond one's right to question, beyond one's capacity to change.[22]

The term "culture shock" has usually been reserved for international travelers who suffer what Enrique Vargas has termed the "jet-age malady." However, in a broad sense, one might compare it to the stories of the African natives who refuse to go so far in one day that their souls cannot catch up with them during the night. In a cultural sense then, "culture shock" would result if the institutions had been outdistanced technologically. It may have been relatively simple for a primitive tribe to accept the innovation of the wheel, for instance. However, the very possibility that modern technology could make what has previously been termed "work" obsolete is causing a wide variety of social repercussions.

In the jet travelers' case, Vargas observes that the shock is "precipitated by the distressing feelings of uncertainty and anxiety that result from not finding all the familiar symbols, signs, and cues that guide a person through his culture."[23] However, the term "culture shock" seems even more appropriate for the modern man who has been attacked from all sides—theologically, cosmically, biologically, psychologically, culturally, and technologically; who has been rendered senseless, lost his image of himself and of his God; and who is now reawakening, trying to reorient himself spatially, temporally, and morally.

This concept of culture shock is even more significant when we consider it in relation to the problem of man's identity in the twentieth century. For, as Vargas suggests, the extent of culture shock which an individual experiences will depend "first of all, upon the amount of change he can experience without having to feel that his sense of personal identity is being threatened; and secondly on his degree of involvement in a foreign experience and how much it differs from what he has been used to."[24]

The image of the secret agent assumes particular importance at this point, not only because of his ability to survive the experience of culture shock on his missions around the world and the blackouts inflicted by his enemies, but also because of his capacity to maintain a sense of identity and integrity despite his anonymity. Consequently this image is as vitally significant for the image of Western man during the tumultuous changes of this century as the image of the medieval knight was for the radical cultural shift which occurred following the Middle Ages. The knight was an identification figure *sine qua non* for the movement into the towns by a group of people who had been ninety percent agrarian, offering the symbol of a man whose allegiance was beyond his family or his land or even his liege-lord. Similarly, since our civilization is moving into a social structure which is rapidly becoming ninety percent urbanized, we need an image of man which can survive in these conditions. The images of the knight and of the secret agent both present hero figures who are required to be "inner directed" in order to survive, who are able to exercise responsible autonomy instead of a sickly heteronomy following the fleeting vagaries of popular fancy. I think we would deceive ourselves if we were to suppose that these figures are not just as "tradition directed" as any other, because most societies produce the type of individual required for survival. But, in this case, tradition requires an image of a strong masculine personality who is able to maintain himself in boundary situations without the customary social support from family and peers. The knight was bound to a rigid code of behavior in his tradition, but the secret agent image reveals the mobility and flexibility required within a fluid social situation.

Since World War II, social scientists have shifted their viewpoints regarding the possibility for man to reorder any society from the ground up, and the individual has been viewed as dwarfed by a multitude of factors beyond his personal control. As Allan Wheelis has stated, it is not possible to view the life of any man apart from the society in which he lives, for "there is no man whose life has not been shaped from birth to death by its cultural matrix."[25] Consequently, since man is a social animal nurtured by the process of socialization, the major question is whether or not a particular society requires and provides support for individual autonomy on a responsible basis.

Actually too many critics of this age are bewailing the dreadful pressures which they believe are directed against the individual. The situation is not quite so simple and is in fact highly contradictory: the mobility and flexibility which are necessary for a highly urbanized, technological society require individuals who are able to survive rapid dislocation and transient situations. The problem is not necessarily just that the individual suffers alienation from his traditional sources of support, for all too often these backgrounds are limiting and alienating in themselves. The problem is that individuals do become so closely attached to the world they have always taken for granted and to the social identity, or "persona," which that world imposed upon them, that any transition may cause culture shock. Unfortunately contemporary society has been forcing these transitions without providing the institutional bases for individual support. In our form of syncopated society which often fails to provide appropriate rites of transition, each individual is forced into a peculiar battle for the survival of the fittest on psycho-sociological terms, such as Durkheim's studies of *anomie* and suicide revealed. Those who are unable to win this battle are lost, unless they can be reoriented within a simpler, more paternalistic type of group, such as the Synanon groups presently offer the dope addict.

In a mass society, each individual faces an attenuated version of the anonymity which is part of the image of the secret agent, particularly the two facets suggested in the television song quoted earlier: first, "to every one he meets, he stays a stranger," and second, "they've given you a number—and taken 'way your name." The anonymity in itself is not the primary issue; for once the conditions of a particular reality are recognized explicitly, man may begin to evaluate which aspects might be changed and which must be accepted. As Viktor Frankl observed concerning the dreadful existence of the prisoners in the Nazi concentration camps:

> . . . any attempt to restore a man's inner strength in the camp had first to succeed in showing him some future goal. Nietzsche's words, "He who has a *why* to live for can bear with almost any *how,*" could be the guiding motto. . . . Whenever there was an opportunity for one, one had to give them a *why*—an aim—for their lives, in order to strengthen them to bear the terrible *how* of their existence. Woe to him who saw no more sense in his life, no aim, no purpose, and therefore no point in carrying on. He was soon lost.[26]

The particular reality which modern man is being shocked into realizing and accepting is the most terrible *how* of man's existence: first, that his destiny is to be alone and to be aware of being alone, and then to be responsible in this new awareness. Anonymity and depersonalization are "dragons" quite justifiably feared in a society whose process of socialization has been based upon other-directedness and heteronomy instead of mutual respect, cooperation, and self-transcendent autonomy. However those dragons are only paper dragons, for identities which can be lost this way were only "paper identities" from the beginning. Although not without cost, we can view their loss then as an occasion for new maturity and responsibility.

One of the most difficult ideas to accept about the process of individuation, however, is that it ultimately leads to a greater sense of community and responsibility, rather than to a blatant sense of individualism and irresponsibility.[27] The process of depersonalization might be considered in a new light—as an extremely painful process which forces the childish ego to drop its "persona," which is the role or mask behind which one plays a social role or game, and to accept its "shadow," which is the hidden aspect of all one would prefer to ignore about one's self. By losing the persona and accepting the shadow, one becomes aware of the wider world and sensitive to its reality and needs. By no longer being enclosed within the petty personal world of an immature ego or limited to the role of a pseudo-self or a paper identity, one then may drop the position of an "actor" in the world and assume the responsibilities of the "agent." The world may then be perceived as a network of social fictions, such as Berger suggests in *The Precarious Vision,* or as a gigantic playing field for the "games people play" (cf. Eric Berne), a world in which one possesses the courage to be and to become. In Paul Tillich's words:

> This is why God Himself cannot liberate man from his aloneness: it is man's greatness that he is centered within himself. Separated from his world, he is thus able to look *at* it. Only because he can look at it can he know and love and transform it. God, in creating him the ruler of the earth, had to separate him and thrust him into aloneness. Man is also therefore able to be spoken to by God and by man. He can ask questions and give answers and make decisions. He has the freedom for good and evil. Only he who has an impenetrable center in himself is freed. Only he who is alone can claim to be a man. This is the greatness and this is the burden of man.[28]

The emergence of the image of the secret agent therefore has a much greater significance than that which might be suggested by box-office receipts or by book-club sales. As a symbol of transformation, it points ahead toward a positive image of man who is able to act creatively and responsibly in the "world come of age." Its appearance not only provides a direct contradiction to the idea that modern man may dispense with myth, but also reveals man's continuing need for fresh symbols to create and sustain community.

005 • The Devil with James Bond!

'Twas brillig, and the slithy toves
  Did gyre and gimble in the wabe:
All mimsy were the borogoves,
  And the mome raths outgrabe.

"Beware the Jabberwock, my son!
  The jaws that bite, the claws that catch!
Beware the Jubjub bird, and shun
  The frumious Bandersnatch!"

He took his vorpal sword in hand:
  Long time the manxome foe he sought. . . .

"Jabberwocky"
Lewis Carroll[1]

"We Scots have a tremendous appreciation of the worlds of the devil." Sean Connery (referring to himself and Ian Fleming)[2]

Put on the whole armor of God, that you may be able to stand against the wiles of the devil. For we are not contending against flesh and blood, but against the principalities, against the powers, against the world rulers of this present darkness, against the spiritual hosts of wickedness in the heavenly places.

Ephesians 6:11-12 (R.S.V.)

What on earth does James Bond have that countless other spies and secret agents do not have?

From one perspective we might admit, "Not much," for one by

one the others can surpass Fleming's secret agent: John Drake (of *Secret Agent*) has presented a far purer image of the secret agent as a hero figure, more akin to the old cowboy prototype—strong, virile, dedicated to restoring single-handedly the balance of good over evil, more inclined to kiss his horse than a girl. Quiller is more intelligent, Peter Trees the Third more elegant, Maxwell Smart more bumbling, Nick Carter more lascivious, Leamas more victimized, Tiger Mann more violent, Matt Helm more cynical, Deighton's agent more realistic, Boysie Oakes more fantastically improbable, and so on. It would be difficult indeed to claim that Bond is remarkable in any of these categories, or that his adventures are representative of good spy literature, which Fleming once suggested should be "full of loose ends and drabness and ultimate despair." He even stated that perhaps only Somerset Maugham, Graham Greene, and Eric Ambler had caught the "squalor and greyness of the Secret Service."[3]

Yet all this merely substantiates Fleming's statements that originally he had never meant Bond to be more than an interesting character to whom extraordinary things happen, an entirely anonymous instrument whom the action of the books would carry along. He admitted that Bond was an "author's pillow fantasy," typical of the adolescent type of mind which he admitted possessing himself. He thought of Bond essentially as a man of action in a violent age, and described him with such adjectives as hard, ruthless, sardonic, fatalistic, sensual, and hedonistic. As he said, "Bond is healthy, detached; disengaged—a sort of amalgam of romantic tough guys, dressed up in twentieth-century clothes, using twentieth-century language. Although I wove around him a great web of excitement and fantasy, I think he is slightly more true to the type of modern heroes—like the spies and commandoes of the last war—than any of the rather cardboard heroes of the old-style thrillers."[4]

If there is nothing particularly unique about Bond even in Fleming's own characterization of him, what then could be outstanding about this particular secret agent? What remains after one eliminates the girls, the guns, the wines, and the cars? In short, what does Bond have which the other agents are missing?

The answer lies in another dimension, for the one thing which Bond has which completely overshadows all the others is his repertory of villains—his honest-to-goodness, larger-than-life villains which he must encounter and destroy! These are extraordinary villains indeed—far from the campy extremes of television's Batman series, for on one hand they are the twentieth-century dragons lying in wait for a twentieth-century St. George, and on the other hand, in the poetic fancies of our subconscious, they are the modern personifications of the devil in new clothes.

By establishing this repertory of villains, with one bold stroke Fleming jumped obliquely across the chessboard of contemporary literature with his twentieth-century knight and commenced the hero quest of this age. With blithe indifference to literary styles and a sincere recognition of the limits of his own literary capabilities, he carried out his peculiar ploy right under the averted noses of critics and commentators who have been longing for such a hero figure. With daring presumption he ignored the fashionable posture of the existentialists who bemoan the loss of meaning in our age of ambiguity. Instead of a man dangling by the puppet strings of contemporary malaise a la Herzog, he has presented a professional capable of mission and responsibility. From a shoddy "world full of grey," Fleming leaped into a technicolor world with a new palette of vivid sins for portraying our times. One by one he carefully set up the false gods of our society just like ducks in a carnival shooting-gallery and then proceeded to knock them down.

Take away the girls and the guns in almost every other secret agent story and there's nothing left but an empty balloon from a neatly configured scheme of intrigue. Take away the girls and the guns from Fleming's saga, tighten up the gaps between the thirteen adventures, and you have a series of hero deeds comparable to those of the Red Cross Knight in Edmund Spenser's *Faerie Queene* or of Bunyan's Christian in *Pilgrim's Progress.* Before investigating this twentieth-century saga, however, we need to examine the peculiar requirements for the hero quest today, a quest which has been proposed on both external (societal) and internal (psychological) bases.

Although most modern men in our syncopated society are much too sophisticated to admit either being afraid of the dark or of the devil, there is one group of social critics who point gloomily to other specters which loom menacingly against the horizon and to social dragons which need slaying. In order to understand this perspective, E. V. Walter suggests that the idea of progress, which was the central myth of the Enlightenment, has become inverted and unrecognized in a new dominant myth of our post-modern age which results in a "familiar bleak fantasy of civilized man trapped in a technological wasteland."[5]

This mood is reflected by the anthropologist Eric Wolf who has suggested that in contrast to the subjective emotional perspective of the humanists, anthropology has become "but a latter-day version of the descent into hell, into a strange and bizarre underworld, in which the hero—disguised as The Investigator—walks untouched among the shades because he carries in his hand the magic sword of Science."[6] He suggests that the cold postwar world is a "world of enormous societies pitted against each other, a world of dinosaurs in which the big lord it over the small, in which the facts of social and cultural dominance are inescapable." In addition to suspecting that there is now much less room for external change in the world, he feels that the cold realities of the postwar world reveal human nature as less flexible than earlier optimists had hoped:

> It is the apparently inherent dilemmas of human existence that strike our consciousness, not the hope of their transcendence. If human nature has set limits, then it also appears changeable only within such limits.[7]

In contrast with this perspective which perceives contemporary dragons to be exterior and social, there is another group of social critics who believe the primary quest of the creative hero to be internal. In *The Hero with a Thousand Faces* Joseph Campbell has portrayed the breakdown of the old symbol systems provided by former mythologies based either upon animal and plant worlds or upon the celestial spheres. He perceives that the problem today consists of "rendering the modern world spiritually significant . . . making it possible for men and women to come to full human maturity through the conditions of contemporary life." He suggests, furthermore, that man himself is now the crucial mystery:

> Man is that alien presence with whom the forces of egoism must come to terms, through whom the ego is to be crucified and resurrected, and in whose image society is to be reformed. Man, understood however not as "I" but as "Thou": for the ideals and temporal institutions of no tribe, race, continent, social class, or century can be the measure of the inexhaustible and multifariously wonderful divine existence that is the life in all of us.[8]

Because of this Campbell believes that the individual cannot wait for society to "cast off its slough of pride, fear, rationalized avarice, and sanctified misunderstandings," but rather the creative hero must begin to guide and direct society.

Similarly, Esther Harding has observed in *Journey into Self* that whenever the collective safeguards of civilization have been undermined, when social and religious dominants begin to decay, individuals are left to grapple with the archetypal symbols themselves and the process of individuation. Much of the powerful public appeal which *Pilgrim's Progress* had during the seventeenth century was derived from its new guidance for the individuals who had been shaken by the disintegration of the former established ways of life provided by feudalism and Catholicism.

This perspective is amplified, moreover, by Stanley Romaine Hopper, who has observed that what we perceive outwardly as a cultural phenomenon of our time is "experienced inwardly as alienation, abandonment, isolation, and solitariness." He suggests therefore that the calling of the poet today is that of alienation and return. "And on the journey he must encounter all the dragons of the inner life, including those let loose by the breaking of the chains of custom." But, even more, since he believes that the "problems of order and of calling today are not merely psychological, but also ethical and religious," Hopper would prefer to state that "modern literature, like St. George, has gone out to capture dragons."[9]

After considering these viewpoints, there is a certain humorous element regarding our analogy between James Bond and St. George. Judging from the great quantity of negative comments about the movie version of James Bond as well as those which we have quoted already from book reviews, it would seem more satisfying for many people to call secret agent 007 the devil himself, instead of the dragon-slayer! Simply for the sake of accuracy, one must admit that there are in fact many points of similarity between Bond and that old prince of demons known as Asmodeus, who was famous (or infamous) for his gambling, his success with women, and his ingenuity and charm as well as for his indictments against social evil.[10] Of course, since Fleming did suggest that perhaps the old list of seven deadly sins might be closer to virtues today, maybe in his perspective we could suggest that old demons could be closer to saints.

However, the point to be made is that the devil has two major tricks, one of which is letting men believe that they have identified him in the wrong place. His other trick is much more subtle, for, as Baudelaire pointed out, "The Devil's cleverest wile is to convince us that he does not exist." The emergence of the new group of death-of-God theologians might easily have been predicted from the earlier demise of the devil. Even though the devil was one of the most persistent characters portrayed in the Bible, today we would have to agree with Denis de Rougemont's perception: "like the Cheshire cat in *Alice in Wonderland,* the Devil has in our day completely disappeared, leaving only a grin hovering in mid-air which is imperceptible to people in a hurry."[11]

The danger which the devil presents to modern man is therefore more insidious than carbon monoxide gas. Just as this deadly gas is twice as effective because it is indiscernible to our sense of smell, so too the devil may act more efficiently because he has tricked us into believing that "nobody but nobody" believes any more in sprightly little red devils with horns—or those in black union-suits with tails and pitchforks—or even those old blue devils of melancholy. This trick is exceptionally efficient, for as de Rougemont comments:

> *Thus, the more he prevails in our lives, the less we are able to recognize him.* The more effective he is, the less danger-

> ous he appears. His own activity conceals him from the eyes of the one it dominates. He vanishes in his success, and his triumph is his incognito.
>
> The proof that the Devil exists, acts and succeeds is precisely that we no longer believe in him.[12]

Because the devil has been so successful in his campaign to convince us that he no longer exists, under the cover of his subsequent anonymity he has gradually been able to enlarge his sphere of operations. His ultimate strategy, of course, is designed to separate man completely from God. Although this campaign appears to be progressing satisfactorily at present, it is linked to several secondary skirmishes. The battle against man's belief in hell has almost been concluded victoriously, and those against the affirmation of this world as God's creation and the realization of individual sin and responsibility have advanced significantly. The one attack which has had a slight reversal lately has been the attempt to eliminate completely man's recognition of his own death. The removal of the elderly and the fatally ill to secluded places for retirement and dying had represented an advance for the devil's side, but he has had to retreat since then following the recent debates over the high cost of many funerals. Unfortunately morticians' attempts to preserve the illusion of "no-death" was becoming too expensive—causing the "Scotch" among us to register a financial protest and consequently giving the theologians a chance to question the drift of men's thinking!

Needless to say, any counterattacks against this sinister, undercover campaign of the devil must be mounted very carefully, because the insulation of contemporary Pharisees has become quite heavy. C. S. Lewis was able to penetrate some of our contemporary defenses several decades ago in his *Screwtape Letters,* but generally anyone attempting to produce a modern version of Dante's *Inferno* with its nine concentric circles of hell would be quickly laughed out of court. Now that the concept of a three-story universe consisting of heaven, earth, and hell has been safely relegated to the categories of outdated myth and metaphor, nobody wants to worry about hell being here and now—unless it is proclaimed at some comfortable distance—at Selma, Alabama, or

Buchenwald and Dachau. Any suggestion that the contemporary battle of Satan's minions against the angels of the Lord is continuing to be waged within some unconscious realm of our own particular soul is blocked out of conscious awareness immediately.

One of the subtle indications which Fleming gave to his readers in order to suggest that he was providing a contemporary descent into hell was the scene in *Moonraker* when Bond was sufficiently surprised by some great crimson words being proclaimed by a gigantic flashing sky-sign that he stopped his car for further investigation. The reader's curiosity is aroused at Bond's amusement when he discovers that a building had merely been blocking out a few letters from a Shell advertisement: "SUMMER SHELL IS HERE." But, with more complete data at hand, we might easily be convinced that Fleming's primary concern is to announce precisely the same pre-apocalyptic message which originally had attracted Bond's attention: "HELL IS HERE . . . HELL IS HERE . . . HELL IS HERE."

One must readily admit that Fleming's version of hell lacks both the grandeur and depth of its portrayal given by Dante and Milton. Nevertheless, his work bears particular significance on several accounts: first, that millions of readers around the world have already been exposed willingly to his symbolism; second, that this symbolism is peculiarly appropriate to the spirit of the times; and third, that, regardless of its literary merits, Fleming's work presents a highly sophisticated theological viewpoint concerning the nature of man. These points deserve particular commendation not only because they reveal that Fleming's personifications of the devil are accurate representations of the temptations which surround us daily, but also because he was able to present very profound concepts in an entertaining fashion on a level of communication available to a vast world audience.

Although other admirers have already commented upon Fleming's abilities to maintain tension in such scenes as the bridge game against Sir Hugo Drax in *Moonraker,* the golf game against Goldfinger, the torturous journey through the tunnels in *Doctor No,* and the ski chase scene in *On Her Majesty's Secret Service,* there has been little comment about the brief, biting scenes of social criticism which represent Fleming's first attack against the "OK" world of today. These scenes range from the satiric portrayal of the sophisticated, sparkling dinner scene at Blades where the elegant diners are surrounded with vulgar scenes of the Hellfire Club (*Moonraker*), the self-righteousness of the health faddists in *Thunderball,* the living graveland of death in St. Petersburg (*Live and Let Die*), the vacuity of the women gamblers in Las Vegas (*Diamonds Are Forever*), the snobbery and pride of those engaged in tracing their family genealogies (*On Her Majesty's Secret Service*) to more savage indictments suggested by the spellbinding scenes with Baron Samedi in *Live and Let Die,* the various modern courts of the devil depicted in the organization meetings of SMERSH, SPECTRE, and the different criminal syndicates, and most particularly the description of Shatterhand's quick efficient "Disneyland of Death" for those desiring more immediate forms of suicide (*You Only Live Twice*). As just one illustration of Fleming's rejection of the cheapness and superficiality of many aspects of contemporary life, we might turn to the comments made by Felix Leiter and Bond concerning St. Petersburg:

> "It makes you want to climb right into the tomb and pull the lid down," said Leiter at Bond's exclamations of horror. . . . Bond groaned. "Let's get away from here," he said. "This is really beyond the call of duty." (LLD, p. 90)

However, these scenes of banality represent only the first level of Fleming's perspective of our modern hell, just as the surface of the sea only masks the activity going on at the deeper levels where his real targets lurk:

> How safe it was, slipping through the night in this ridiculously vulnerable little boat. How kind and soft the sea could be. . . . Bond thought of what was going on in the hundreds of fathoms below the boat, the big fish, the shark and barracuda and tarpon and sailfish quietly cruising, the shoals of kingfish and mackerel and bonito and, far below in the grey twilight of the great depths, the phosphorous jellied boneless things that were never seen, the fifty-foot squids, with eyes a foot wide, that streamed along like zeppelins, the last real monsters of the sea, whose size was only known from the

> fragments found inside whales. What would happen if a wave caught the canoe broadside and capsized them? How long would they last? (DN, pp. 66-67)

The primary action of the Bond series is centered therefore upon those intangible representatives of the devil who are lurking anonymously in the shades just beyond the borders of our conscious attention. One by one Fleming has snared these monsters within his nets and dragged them out where they may no longer remain incognito; one by one they may be counted off in Fleming's own book about the devil and his disciples. By examining them, accordingly, we may be able, as Bond had wished in *Casino Royale,* to "learn the nature of evil in all its forms, with parables about evil people, proverbs about evil people, folklore about evil people"!

One of the first suspicions we might have regarding Fleming's modern repertory of demons is that possibly they could reflect his revised perspective concerning the nature of the seven deadly sins. As we have seen earlier, in his introduction to *The Seven Deadly Sins,* Fleming had suggested that being possessed of the ancient seven (Envy, Pride, Covetousness, Gluttony, Sloth, Lust, and Anger) one might still go to heaven, whereas he believed that "to be afflicted by the modern variations can only be a passport to hell." His revised list of what he termed the seven deadlier sins, therefore, had included Avarice, Cruelty, Snobbery, Hypocrisy, Self-Righteousness, Moral Cowardice, and Malice. In addition, on the side he also included Sloth in its extreme form of accidie, as the only one of the original seven which would have his own wholehearted condemnation. If Fleming did use this new list of deadlier sins for the personification of the devil in modern dress, his work would be entirely congruent with such earlier English moralists as Chaucer, Langland, Bunyan, and Spenser, all of whom had included the earlier lists of sins in various forms for their own generations.

However, by doing so, Fleming would provide a remarkable addition to the field of English literature, because Morton W. Bloomfield has suggested in his exhaustive study of the seven deadly sins that Spenser's work has been considered to be the last great treatment of the sins. As Bloomfield points out, since Spenser the concept of these sins has not died out, "but it was never again to occupy an important part in life and culture. The *tradition* of the Sins was dead; they no longer evolved; they no longer inspired great writing."[13]

It is already apparent from Fleming's list of revised sins not only that he is interested in restoring both the concept and the tradition of the sins, but also that in his work the sins have evolved and do reflect the changing circumstances of our generation. In addition, we may even suggest that perhaps his versions are more fully characterized than those of his predecessors. For example we can point to the long confessional scenes between Bond and his villains. These long dialogues far surpass the simpler confessional scene in which the various sins speak out in their own voices in Langland's *Piers Plowman,* a scene which Bloomfield has considered to be the greatest treatment of the cardinal sins in English literature because of its "masterly combination of the abstract and the specific."

In illustration of this point, by rapidly running down Fleming's list of the "seven deadlier sins," it is quite obvious that Goldfinger is an outstanding elaboration of the evils of Avarice. In their first meeting, Bond is impressed by Goldfinger's relaxed attitude, which "showed in the economy of his movement, of his speech, of his expressions. Mr. Goldfinger wasted no effort, yet there was something coiled, compressed, in the immobility of the man." Immediately thereafter, however, Bond is repelled by Goldfinger's grotesque, "out of proportion" appearance and proceeds to give a very Adlerian type of psychoanalysis of how Goldfinger got to be the villain that he is. Later in the book, Goldfinger's own confession is a masterful revelation of the motivation impelling the actions of a modern Midas:

> "Mr. Bond—" For the first time since Bond had known Goldfinger, the big, bland face, always empty of expression, showed a trace of life. A look almost of rapture illuminated the eyes. The finely chiselled lips pursed into a thin, beatic curve. "Mr. Bond, all my life I have been in love. I have

> been in love with gold. I love its colour, its brilliance, its divine heaviness. I love the texture of gold, that soft sliminess that I have learnt to gauge so accurately by touch that I can estimate the fineness of a bar to within one carat. And I love the warm tang it exudes when I melt it down into a true golden syrup. But, above all, Mr. Bond, I love the power that gold alone gives to its owner—the magic of controlling energy, exacting labour, fulfilling one's every wish and whim and, when need be, purchasing bodies, minds, even souls. Yes, Mr. Bond I have worked all my life for gold and in return, gold has worked for me and for those enterprises that I have espoused. I ask you," Goldfinger gazed earnestly at Bond, "is there any other substance on earth that so rewards its owner?" (p. 135)

Although such long confessional speeches are presented by all the most evil of Fleming's villains directly, in several other cases he allows other characters to present external judgments concerning the nature of particular sins. For example, although the sin of Snobbery is represented in its extreme by the Count de Bleuville in *On Her Majesty's Secret Service* (actually Blofeld in disguise), the major speeches against snobbery and vanity are given by Sable Basilisk as he briefs Bond on his cover story. The health faddists in *Thunderball* illustrate the sin of Self-Righteousness most satirically, and even "M" and Bond succumb to this type of temptation temporarily. Although it is possible to suggest that Sir Hugo Drax (*Moonraker*) illustrates Moral Cowardice, since he commits the dreadful act of cheating at cards, actually Darko Kerim's speech in *From Russia with Love* strikes more deeply into the hidden implications of this sin, because he reveals the mistake of falsely assuming the laws of any earthly game are ultimate. Although all of Fleming's villains present varying degrees of Malice and Cruelty, these sins are most diabolically represented by the villainess, Rosa Klebb, the sadistic mother figure who specializes in human torture and whom Fleming describes a la Whistler's mother in the conclusion of *From Russia with Love*.

In addition, many of Fleming's villains personify Hypocrisy, for they attempt to deceive the general public by appearing under the cover of decent law-abiding citizens. Superficially Jack

Spang (*Diamonds Are Forever*) is a model citizen, but actually he directs the operations of an evil syndicate responsible for a vast network of organized crime, ranging from bookmaking, narcotics, and organized prostitution to smuggling diamonds. Although ostensibly Sir Hugo Drax has gained the stature of one of Britain's new national heroes, underneath this superficial facade of a gentleman of propriety he actually is obsessed by the desire for revenge against his Fatherland's enemies and secretly is plotting to bomb London.

As we continue to examine Fleming's villains more carefully, we begin to recognize also that they are not only representations of his list of "seven deadlier sins," but that their descriptions also present a historical progression of the characteristic descriptions regarding the devil. His first archfiend, Mister Big (*Live and Let Die*), personifies one of the earliest forms of the demonic for he is a black devil. According to Maximilian Rudwin, a black face was a permanent feature of the medieval representations of the devil, and in Scotland today it is still a common belief that the Devil is a black man.

Four of the later villains possess another typical characteristic of the devil, red hair: Sir Hugo Drax, Red Grant, Goldfinger, and Scaramanga. With a completely bald head, however, Doctor No is typical of the tradition of the devil as long, lean, bald, and cadaverous. Since Blofeld completely changes his appearance two times from one book to the next, his personification is not only typical of the "blues" version of the devil, but also that of Archimago in Spenser's *Faerie Queene,* which parallels that traditional concept of the devil's amazing ability to assume a variety of forms. As opposed to all of the "larger-than-life" type villains, the figure of Scaramanga in the last book presents an incongruous letdown, unless one suspects that he represents the most contemporary identification of the devil as just man himself, a latter-day Adam who is depicted consuming the serpent in the middle of a modern Garden of Evil.

All of these analyses are incomplete, however, for they fail to account for Fleming's statements regarding Sloth, accidie, which he said had his wholehearted condemnation, perhaps because in moments of despair he had "seen its face." As we have noticed earlier, he had defined this sin as a form of "spiritual suicide" and a "refusal of joy," which is a return to the original monastic and ascetic understanding of accidie as spiritual dryness rather than the medieval and puritanical concept of sloth as mere laziness.

That accidie continued to be Fleming's prime concern is evident as we examine the entire series. In doing so, we see that the specter of accidie is constantly revealing its face to the reader in a variety of forms. In a mild version it is present in two of the minor villains, Emilio Largo, who made a "fetish of inertia," and Rosa Klebb, whose besetting vice was a laziness combined with a psychological and physiological neutrality which was able to relieve her of "so many human emotions and sentiments and desires."

However, the face of accidie is presented with greatest force in the descriptions and confessions of Fleming's three major villians: Mister Big, Doctor No, and Blofeld. As the first of this demonic trio, Mister Big represents the aesthete, who states that he is suffering from "boredom or accidie," because he is able to take pleasure only in artistry, in polish and finesse, and who is impelled by a mania to "impart an absolute rightness, a high elegance, to the execution of his affairs," each day setting "higher standards of subtlety and technical polish so that each of [his] proceedings may be a work of art."

The second, on the other hand, is the technician, as represented by Doctor No, who is characterized by a "supreme indifference" and a mania for power—"to do unto others what had been done unto [him], the power of life and death, the power to decide, to judge, the power of absolute independence from outside authority . . . the essence of temporal power." He agrees with Bond that power itself is an illusion, but adds, "So is beauty, Mister Bond. So is art, so is money, so is death. And so, probably, is life." He confesses that in his early years he "loved the death and destruction of people and things," and now, in addition to his other diabolical plans, he is engaged in experiments to determine how much the human body can endure. As he says, "You see,

Mister Bond, I am interested in the anatomy of courage—in the power of the human body to endure. But how to measure human endurance? How to plot a graph of the will to survive, the tolerance of pain, the conquest of fear?"

The most imposing personification of accidie, however, is the one presented in the third and most demonic version by the figure of Blofeld, specifically in his last characterization as "Shatterhand" in *You Only Live Twice.* In his final encounter scene with Bond at his Castle of Death, he appears as a modern version of Giant Despair, dressed in a "magnificent black silk kimono across which a golden dragon sprawled" and proceeds to deliver the ultimate apologia for Sloth, as he explains his demonic "Disneyland of Death":

> I will make a confession to you, Mister Bond. I have come to suffer from a certain lassitude of mind which I am determined to combat. This comes in part from being a unique genius who is alone in the world, without honour—worse, misunderstood. No doubt much of the root cause of this accidie is physical—liver, kidneys, heart, the usual weak points of the middle-aged. But there has developed in me a certain mental lameness, a disinterest in humanity and its future, an utter boredom with the affairs of mankind. So, not unlike the gourmet, with his jaded palate, I now seek only the highly spiced, the sharp impact on the taste buds, mental as well as physical, the tickle that is truly exquisite. And so, Mister Bond, I came to devise this useful and essentially humane project—the offer of free death to those who seek release from the burden of being alive. (pp. 216-217)

After a vicious battle, first by Bond's stave against Blofeld's sword and then hand to hand, Bond is able to destroy this version of Giant Despair and blow up his Doubting Castle. And at this point, many themes begin to converge. Not only does James Bond represent a modern St. George, but the primary dragon or devil which he must battle is that of the capital sin of our generation, the sin of sloth, the accidie which is a refusal of life and joy, the utter indifference, carelessness, and inertia—in short, the feeling of apathy with which we began this study.

The face of accidie is the face which is haunting both social scientists and theologians, but it is also the monster which is threatening to choke our civilization. In *From Russia with Love* Fleming states at one point that the "blubbery arms of the soft life had Bond around the neck and they were slowly strangling him." A little later he allows a curious quotation to slip into Bond's mind: "Those whom the Gods wish to destroy, they first make bored."

Since Bond's fight is our fight as well, in the next chapter we need to explore the various dimensions of the struggle against accidie—that enemy which the theologians would call sloth and the social scientist would term apathy.

006 • "Where's the Action?"

> The curse of America is sheer, hopeless, well-ordered boredom; and that is going someday to be the curse of the world.
>
> Rudyard Kipling

> People no longer seem to know why they are alive; existence is simply a string of near-experiences marked off by a period of stupifying spiritual and psychological stasis, and the good life is basically an amused one. . . . Standing around with nothing coming up is as close to dying as you can get. Unless one grasps the power of boredom, the threat of it to one's existence, it is impossible to "place" the delinquent as a member of the human race.
>
> Arthur Miller[1]

> The worst sin towards our fellow creatures is not to hate them, but to be indifferent to them: that's the essence of inhumanity.
>
> *The Devil's Disciple*
> George Bernard Shaw

> "And to the angel of the church in Laodicea write: . . . 'I know your works; you are neither cold nor hot. Would that you were cold or hot! So, because you are lukewarm, and neither cold nor hot, I will spew you out of my mouth. For you say, I am rich, I have prospered, and I need nothing; not knowing that you are wretched, pitiable, poor, blind and naked. . . .' "
>
> Revelation 3:14-17 (R.S.V.)

The interesting advantage which we have in adapting the legend of St. George and the dragon to the contemporary problem of accidie or apathy is that it speaks so eloquently to our situation. Why did the villagers capitulate so readily to the dragon's demands? Why did they allow temporary expediency to result in the sacrifice of their children? Why did they ignore the Roman precept: *Principiis obsta* (Resist the beginnings)? The villagers themselves may be said to symbolize the inertia inherent in group action, the phenomenon of public apathy and the prevalent response of "Let George do it!" And, even though our dragon today is an apathy threatening to poison our entire society, it is just because the problem is so acute and yet presents such an intangible force, that it is able to produce the same numbed reaction within our society that the original dragon did among the villagers so long ago.

The one minor detail missing from the early legend which would need to be added today to complete the imagery would be a study committee of scientists and theologians who would begin analyzing the destructive power of the dragon and begin recommending possible countermeasures to combat its deadly effects. In the meantime, however, due to cultural expediency, the young people would continue to be sacrificed in lieu of the entire society. Even though the dragon known as apathy is intangible, its handiwork is obvious to careful observers.

Probably the most vociferous of the many commentators who have been examining the problem of apathy have been those social scientists and therapists forced to deal with its victims daily. These experts generally consider it a symptom of psychological malaise due to various forms of cultural dysfunction. They relate it to a host of associated symptoms, in a manner which could be compared to the grasping tentacles of the giant squid—boredom and the incapacity for leisure, "anomie" (normlessness) and despair leading to suicide, juvenile delinquency and public apathy, the decline of the superego and the increase of moral cowardice, all of which combine to produce a syndrome of decay and death.

The most petrifying conclusions which may be drawn from serious research and experience is that apathy is the inevitable monster haunting urban life, whether it cripples those imprisoned by the hopeless despair of the slums, smothers those surfeited by affluence in the suburbs, or reduces all those in between into the faceless anonymity of the masses. A wide variety of writers point to the vicious cycle of urban life, with its cacophony of noises and the incessant drain of nervous energy. Periods of stimulation and boredom are seen oscillating with ever-increasing intensity: first, the search for greater excitement and thrills, followed by an inevitable letdown from satiation, the deadening of affect and perceptions. Those who are able to escape this vicious alternating current all too often are magnetized by an even deadlier direct current, illustrated by the frantic busyness of those unable to find pleasure either in work or leisure, who are constantly on the go and never able to relax. Their motto: "Where's the action?"

There is an almost prophetic ring to the indictments being made by many of these secular authorities. In his comprehensive survey of the history of cities, *Babylon Is Everywhere,* Wolf Schneider concludes that weariness and disgust are the inevitable consequence of city life. V. S. Pritchett, while examining the temptations of boredom, points out that that phenomenon, which was once termed the royal sickness of kings, has now become the central sickness of industrial man. Erich Fromm perceives that indifference to life is an inevitable reaction to an ever-increasing industrialism. Allan Wheelis attributes the vague, all-pervasive uneasiness of many individuals seeking personal therapy to the decline of the superego and the subsequent loss of a sense of meaning. Bruno Bettelheim suggests that the seduced passivity and dependency induced by an all-powerful bureaucracy cannot help discouraging men from facing life actively, which results in the atrophy of the decision-making capability and the failure of responsible autonomy.

In addition to these secular prophets whose observations are generally limited to the discussions of symptoms and syndromes, there are others who have begun to correlate such perceptions with more theological insights. For example, Dr. Karl Menninger has recognized the intangible factors affecting mental and emotional health. In his book, *The Vital Balance,* he suggests that both skeptics and believers can be united on one side against their common enemy which is evil:

> Evil goes in many guises and is called by many names. Perhaps the best name for it is the old-fashioned personi-

> fication, the Devil. It has two faces—the destructiveness itself, with the suffering and loss it causes, and the indifference to it of those more fortunate.[2]

He is particularly concerned over what he terms the "complacency of the comfortable," for he sees this as the "indifference, the apathy, the hardness of heart which troubles neither to believe nor to doubt, but simply does not care." In addition, he would join Norman Cousins in the conviction that our greatest enemy today is not "some powerful nation or totalitarian power controlling world ideology," but rather (in Cousins' words):

> . . . the man whose only concern about the world is that it stay in one piece *during his own lifetime* . . . up to his hips in success . . . [who] not only believes in his own helplessness, but actually worships it [assuming] that there are mammoth forces at work which the individual cannot comprehend much less alter or direct.[3]

In a similar manner, the sociologist Robert K. Merton has stated that the syndrome of "anomie," cultural normlessness, which has been of particular interest to sociologists ever since Durkheim, is related directly to the phenomenon which for centuries the church had identified as the sin of "accidie," the sloth or torpor which indicates that the "wells of the spirit run dry."[4]

This relationship is clarified when we examine R. M. MacIver's definition of *anomy* (his spelling) as the state of mind of one "who has been pulled up by his moral roots, who has no longer any standards but only disconnected urges, who has no longer any sense of continuity, of folk, of obligation." He sees the anomic man as one who has become "spiritually sterile, responsive only to himself, responsible to no one. He derides the values of other men. His only faith is the philosophy of denial. He lives on the thin line of sensation between no future and no past."[5]

From these statements it is obvious how the spirit of apathy threatens modern man, but a historical review of the phenomenon reveals that inertia and indifference constantly have been among man's most persistent enemies. The word "accidie" itself meant "carelessness" and was used most often to condemn those who failed to bury the dead. It is used in this sense in both the *Iliad* and *Odyssey,* but it assumes the additional meaning of leaving one's possessions or guests uncared for as well. Hippocrates uses this word in one of his medical books and, in a letter to Atticus in 45 B.C., Cicero expressed his concern over the latter's "acedia." Moreover, the term was used within the Septuagint, in both Psalm 119:28 and Isaiah 61:3 where it expresses a "faint heart" or a deep "spirit of heaviness."

Despite these many illustrations of the awareness of the problem of accidie, it is the unique recognition of the Christian faith that indifference to life is actually one of the seven deadly sins, a symptom of the loss of faith. This Christian perception stands in direct contradiction to several philosophies of life as well, not only to the Stoic conception of a noble apathy with which the ideal, virtuous, wise man faced life, but also the Epicurean form of serenity, which manifested itself in the avoidance of pain in the search for pleasure as the highest and only good.

It is in Christianity that we see the boldest attack launched against the syndrome of decay and death which is initiated by the capital or source sin of accidie. In Christ men were called out of their encapsulated selves, invited to turn around (repent) and greet the Kingdom of Heaven near at hand. They were called out from a pathological preoccupation with law and guilt, from an endless quest for self-achieved righteousness, from a living death, and invited into a life full of joy, grace, love, and hope. Jesus pointed out that a thief comes only to steal and kill and destroy, but that he had come so that men might have life and have it abundantly. He implored men to give up the self which the world bestows and to find their true selves in him. In the parable of the servants, he proclaimed that those who were faithful with the talents entrusted to them would enter into the joy of their master, while the wicked and slothful servant who lacked courage to invest the money would be condemned and cast into outer darkness.

However, within the New Testament, it is the word "compassion" which provides the most direct contradiction to the spirit of apathy. Although there are at least five Greek words used to indicate compassion, the one which is transliterated as *splagchnizomai* is the one used in the parables of the Prodigal Son and the Good Samaritan:

> *Luke 10:33-34:* But a Samaritan, as he journeyed, came to where he was; and when he saw him, he had *compassion,* and went to him and bound up his wounds, pouring on oil and wine; then he set him on his own beast and brought him to an inn, and took care of him.
> *Luke 15:20:* And he arose and came to his father. But while he was yet at a distance, his father saw him and had *compassion,* and ran and embraced him and kissed him.

Now this particular Greek word is not a namby-pamby word. Instead it is intended to portray a completely visceral reaction to the situation depicted. In completely vernacular terms, it denotes a "gut-level" response, for literally it means to "have one's bowels yearning." It was not used only in these parables, but it was also the word used in the Synoptic Gospels to describe Jesus' reactions to the needs of persons around him—the hungry crowd (Mark 8:1-9), the blind men (Matt. 20:29-34), the leper (Mark 1:40-42), and an epileptic boy (Mark 9:14-29). It applied not only to the times when he was on the road, but also to the times of his own deep grief:

> *Matthew 9:35-36:* And Jesus went about all the cities and villages, teaching in their synagogues and preaching the gospel of the kingdom, and healing every disease and every infirmity. When he saw the crowds, he had *compassion* for them, because they were harassed and helpless, like sheep without a shepherd.
> *Matthew 14:13-14:* Now when Jesus heard this [about the death of his cousin John the Baptist], he withdrew from there in a boat to a lonely place apart. But when the crowds heard it, they followed him on foot from the towns. As he went ashore he saw a great throng; and he had *compassion* on them, and healed their sick.

This compassion, however, which Christ demonstrated in healing those broken in spirit and body was not limited merely to restoring a simple status quo. The book of Mark presents Jesus' constant battle against all of the evil forces which seek to destroy men and to separate them from the love of God. The progression of Christ's struggle against the demonic may be illustrated on several levels: the cosmic dimension in the story of his temptation by the devil in the wilderness when his power through the Holy Spirit was first demonstrated; the personal dimension in the series of exorcism narratives in which he drives out those demons holding individuals in bondage; the historical dimension of the debates with the Jewish authorities in which he is depicted not only acting in history but also seeking to clarify its meaning. James M. Robinson has pointed out that the pervasive trend in Mark, therefore, is to associate Jesus' words with his action:

> . . . for Mark the authority of Jesus' teaching resides not in its force of logic or the originality and profundity of its contents, but rather in the power inherent in him as Son of God and bearer of the Spirit, a power which is revealed by the efficacy of his word. When he speaks, God acts: in casting out a demon, in healing a paralytic, in forgiving sin, in addressing his people at worship. . . . For Jesus' word is action.[6]

The climax of Jesus' victory over the demonic, however, is not manifested until after the crucifixion and resurrection, when at last its power is decisively broken and the power of God's will for man is established in history. For more than a thousand years it was this simple idea of the Atonement which gave Jesus' disciples and followers the courage to act in the conviction of God's grace and power in history. In Christ men were freed from the idea of a cosmic power of evil and consequently able to perceive it as clearly contrary to God's sovereignty over the entire universe. Sin, evil, and death were henceforth subordinate images of all that which God has excluded from his will for mankind; love, grace, and joy were signs of his continuing love and redemption. In Christ the old man Adam lost his vitality and a new Adam was born. Men were called to be the heirs of the Kingdom of Heaven with Christ, no longer slaves to sin or bond servants of the law, but responsible in the world and intended to work out their salvation with "fear and trembling" and the power of the Holy Spirit. Karl Barth has probably given the most emphatic recognition to this distinction in a discussion on the sloth and misery of man. He states:

> The direction of God, given in the resurrection of Jesus Christ who was crucified for us, discloses who is overcome in His death. It is the man who would not make use of his freedom, but was content with a low level of a self-enclosed being, thus being irremediably and radically and totally subject to his own stupidity, inhumanity, dissipation and anxiety, and delivered up to his own death.[7]

It is here then that the essential meaning of the sin of accidie becomes most clear. It is a symptom not only of spiritual aridity but the loss of the whole meaning of salvation. It is the opposite of the process which used to be called "sanctification" by earlier theologians. According to Paul Tillich's analysis, the process of sanctification should mean increasing growth in four areas: first, the increasing awareness of the world around us, which leads to the power of affirming life despite its ambiguities; second, the increasing freedom from the letter of the law, which leads to the power to "judge the given situation in the light of the Spiritual Presence and to decide upon adequate action"; third, increasing relatedness which means not only relating to one's self in solitude but also to others in community; and fourth, increasing self-transcendence, which means a deeper, more mature relationship with God.[8]

It is only with recent years therefore that the various perspectives of social scientists, philosophers, and theologians have begun to converge in their opinions about the question of accidie: the only major difference perhaps being that the secular writers would prefer to use the term "syndrome" for the various aspects of the problem which theologians would call "sin." Harvey Cox has suggested that apathy is the key form of sin in today's world. Joseph Pieper has stated that despair and the incapacity for leisure are twins, that leisure is "only possible when a man is at one with himself, when he acquiesces in his own being, whereas the essence of *acedia* is the refusal to acquiesce in one's own being." Esther Harding has commented upon the numerous occasions in *Pilgrim's Progress* when Christian encountered sloth: in person in the Slough of Despond and the Doubting Castle of the Giant Despair, and in other figures from the man in the iron cage (despair) to Sloth himself. She states that sloth is "perhaps the most fundamental and deep-seated urge of the psyche," and that it often "blocks the way to any change, and especially to that transformation process through which the purely animal man may evolve into a self-aware, conscious personality composed of spirit as well as body." She relates the phenomenon of depression to sloth and the "deliberate choice of ease," and believes that it is a "moral problem with which it was necessary to struggle as against a giant or dragon."[9]

This shift in thinking about accidie and apathy bears a distinct correlation to the conversation between the two characters, Augustine and Franciscus, in Petrarch's *Secretum*. Morris West has provided a new fresh translation of this work written by a man who has been called the father of the Renaissance and who struggled with the problem of accidie six hundred years ago. Franciscus complains about his depression but admits that this plague gives him a certain kind of "atrocious black satisfaction." Everything he sees, hears, and feels afflicts him, and he blames it upon his life within the city. Augustine, who is really Petrarch's more mature self, rejects Franciscus' self-pity and claims that by his own free will he could escape from the two golden chains which fetter him, his vain desire for love and glory. He questions the purpose of Franciscus' labors and fervent studies, and states, ". . . you already know all that is needful for life and death. It would be better for you to apply what you know to your conduct." He concludes by calling upon Franciscus to surrender all of his works, to given himself back to himself, and to begin to think deeply about death.[10]

Accidie therefore is the refusal not only of joy, but the refusal of the new life made possible in Christ. Kierkegaard saw it as the "despairing refusal to be oneself," when one cannot give his consent to his own being or be at one with himself. It is the rejection of the promise of being born again, a sterile stillborn condition in which one continues in the helplessness of sin and guilt from which Christ had fought to redeem mankind. Since basically therefore it is the rejection of God's love in Christ, it inevitably results in defective love for others as well as for oneself. It manifests itself either in an utter indifference to others or in a busy, shallow "works-righteousness" which fails to perceive others or to relate to them.

Just as Ivan Karamazov then, we see the slothful "handing God back his ticket" to life. As Karl Olssen suggests, the slothful is the "no-care, waving away existence with a gesture of the hand; he is the Bored."[11] Or, as James Pike and Howard A. Johnson indicate, the slothful is working "like the devil" because he

> hasn't worked to live; he has lived to work. He has, in fact, had no other life. Like all slothful people, he's bored with life, afraid of life. His own life is empty, so he works in the effort to fill up that big void.[12]

The slothful, therefore, are those incapable of leisure, of the sense of wonder for life and the creative activities which bring new forms of beauty and charm to existence. Instead they are on an endless treadmill, seeking for pleasure which they never seem to find, caught up in a pseudo-good life which is basically unreal, a paper-doll world of only two dimensions—as long as boredom and as wide as despair. As Arthur Miller points out, their good life is the "life of ceaseless entertainment, effortless joys, the air-conditioned, dust-free languor beyond the Müsselman's most supine dream. Freedom is, after all, comfort; sexuality is a photograph. The enemy of it all is the real. The enemy is conflict. The enemy, in a word, is life."[13]

There is only one possible antidote, therefore, for the sin of accidie—the slap into awareness by the real encounter with death. It is for this reason that the spirit of apathy and boredom disappears during wartime and other occasions of crisis when men are forced to re-evaluate the fundamental premises for their existence. The recognition of this aspect of the problem was suggested in the mock haiku poem which Bond composes in Fleming's next-to-last book:

You only live twice:
Once when you are born,
And once when you look death in the face.

It is important to realize, however, that although men may learn to treasure life as they begin to see it slipping from their fingers, it is the Christian conviction that enables men not to fear death as life's enemy but rather to transcend it with the power of love. It is Christ who reminds men: "This night your soul is required of you!"

007 • From Bond to Bonhoeffer

Leiter to Bond: "Maybe you can strike a blow for Freedom, Home and Beauty with that rusty old equalizer of yours." (DF, p. 90)

Bonhoeffer: Yet our business now is to replace our rusty swords with sharp ones.[1]

"Do not think that I have come to bring peace on earth; I have not come to bring peace, but a sword." Matthew 10:34 (R.S.V.)

For the word of God is living and active, sharper than any two-edged sword, piercing to the division of soul and spirit, of joints and marrow, and discerning the thoughts and intentions of the heart. Hebrews 4:12 (R.S.V.)

A rather poignant description of our times was given recently by Arthur Miller. In an article entitled "The Bored and the Violent" he expressed his concern over the problem of juvenile delinquency, which he considers to be "our most notable and violent manifestation of social nihilism." Most solutions for this problem, however, he viewed as "spiritless" for "they do not assume that the wrong is deep and terrible and general among us all. There is, in a word, a spirit gone." Although he could suggest no way to recapture this spirit himself, he described it with remarkable accuracy:

I do not know how we ought to reach for the spirit again but it seems to me we must flounder without it. It is the spirit which does not accept injustice complacently and yet does not betray the poor with sentimentality. It is the spirit which seeks not to flee the tragedy which life must always

> be, but seeks to enter into it, thereby to be strengthened by the fullest awareness of its pain, its ultimate non sequitur. It is the spirit which does not mask but unmasks the true function of a thing, be it business, unionism, architecture, or love.[2]

Although Ian Fleming was never quite as explicit about his concern for today's youth, there are many instances in his work which suggest that his awareness of the situation parallels that of Arthur Miller. In one passage in *Thunderball,* for example, after describing the cheap self-assertiveness of a foxy, pimpled young taxi driver, he allows his secret agent to reflect about the boy's situation:

> This youth, thought Bond, makes about twenty pounds a week, despises his parents, and would like to be Tommy Steele. It's not his fault. He was born into the buyers' market of the Welfare State and into the age of atomic bombs and space flight. For him, life is easy and meaningless. (p. 13)

Most of Fleming's direct comments about the problem of juvenile delinquency per se, however, may be found in one of his secondary books, *Thrilling Cities,* which is a series of thirteen "mood pieces" about the "world's most exciting, exotic and sinful cities." Although this travelogue contains many passages of charming insights into various people and cultures, for the most part it is a gloomy, understated survey of our rather shabby world and the depressing outlook for today's youth. There is a delightful irony about the book consequently, because the sins which Fleming chose to depict are generally not the ones the casual reader would be looking for, but ones which are akin to his list of the "seven deadlier sins."

Besides exposing the tawdry lingerie hidden beneath the glamorous skirts of many cities, Fleming also provides a series of quick deft sketches highlighting the problems of international crime, escapist drugs, moral hypocrisy, the dehumanizing aspects of much modern architecture, and the decline of moral standards. He specifically quotes the four reasons for juvenile delinquency which had been listed in 1959 by the Los Angeles chief of police

—in short, the decline and fall of former values, the direct influences of adult criminality, the increasing emphasis of our society upon materialism without effort, and our attempt to substitute scientific proficiency for social responsibility.[3] Most specifically, however, upon his return from a globe-encircling trip of thirty days, he raises the specific question of why British influence has disappeared so rapidly over half the globe and suggests that the situation can be reversed only by rekindling the "spirit of adventure" so that "our youth can heave itself off its featherbed and stream out and off across the world again."[4]

Although Arthur Miller and Ian Fleming have pointed to two aspects of a spirit which seems to be missing today, there is another dimension of this spirit which we might term that aspect of true iconoclasm which is able to puncture not only our personal pretensions of pride, pomposity, and false piety, but also those false images which we have set up for contemporary idol-worship. It is able to unmask such hypocrisy and delusions of grandeur, but it does not absolve us from responsibility and action. Although initially the image of the "iconoclast" might suggest a negative concept of one who attacks cherished beliefs as sham, it really should indicate the rejection of the religious use of images, one who opposes idolatry in every form.

In his book *Wait Without Idols,* Gabriel Vahanian has pointed out that iconoclasm is the essential ingredient of monotheism and suggests that true iconoclasm "begins with oneself, with the smashing of one's own idols, i.e. one's superannuated conception of God, of faith and religious allegiance."[5] This concept may be further clarified by Richard Niebuhr's studies of radical monotheism, for he states:

> When the principle of being is God, then He alone is holy and ultimate sacredness must be denied to any special being. No special places, times, persons, or communities are more representative of the One than any others are. No sacred groves or temples, no hallowed kings or priests, no festival days, no chosen communities are particularly representative of Him in whom all things live and move and have their being.[6]

As we begin to tie these various perceptions together in relation to the various discussions regarding accidie in previous chapters, it is only natural to suggest that the spirit which seems to be missing in Western civilization is that of the image of St. George. Certainly for centuries this image was able to capture the imagination of countless generations of youth. We can point to a variety of evidence which may be used to suggest that the loss of the spirit of strength and courage exemplified by St. George may result in the growth of boredom and apathy.

Chaucer, for example, gave one of the strongest indications of this relationship in his *Canterbury Tales* when the Parson states that the virtue of *fortitudo* (strength) was the essential remedy against what he termed the "horrible sin of acedia." Terming this sin the enemy of man in every condition and the source of all despair, carelessness, and "that dull coldness that freezes the heart of man," he saw that, in its ultimate degree, "acedia" would produce not only lack of devotion, but also the sin of worldly sorrow (*tristicia*) which he stated would slay man: "For, verily, such sorrow works the death of the soul and of the body also; for thereof it comes to pass that a man is bored by his own life." He perceived *fortitudo* therefore as the virtue which could conquer this sin because of its various aspects of magnanimity, faith, and hope which could give man the force of character to despise annoying things. He saw this virtue as

> so mighty and so vigorous that it dares to withstand sturdily, and wisely to keep itself from dangers that are wicked, and to wrestle against the assaults of the Devil. For it enhances and strengthens the soul, just as acedia reduces it and makes it feeble.[7]

Certainly if it is the case that it is the image of St. George which our culture has been missing, it is necessary to begin to ask just how we managed to lose its dynamic power and how in turn we might begin to recapture it. Might it be possible that the justifiable zeal of Reformation leaders to eliminate the idolatry of saints has somehow backfired? that the Reformers may have failed to liberate the images which had motivated the actions of early saints and instead only succeeded in making possible a more shallow worship of celebrity gods, the idolatry of sport heroes and movie stars, the cults of Superman, Batman, and the robot Eighth Man? Is it possible that all of the well-intentioned efforts to clean up children's literature has somehow unwittingly resulted in more harm than good? Lewis Mumford has already pointed out that we may have fooled ourselves

> when we thought that any antiseptic efforts of ours to keep the germs of fantasy from incubating, could banish the child's sense of the mysterious, the inscrutable, the terrible, the overwhelming. In repressing this life of fantasy and subordinating it to our own practical interests, we perhaps made it take more devious forms, or at least gave the demonic a free hand without conjuring up any angelic powers to fight on the other side. We did not get rid of the dragon; we only banished St. George.[8]

Regardless of the various reasons which might ultimately be assigned for the explanation of the loss of the St. George imagery, it is important to recognize that its power had resulted from the blending of the courageous action of a specific historic person with the dynamic imagery of an already existing myth. As such, it was then able to capture the imagination of many people, not because they were interested in it as an intellectual abstraction of some ethical principle, but because they could identify with the person involved. This tradition of transferring the dynamic characteristics of myth to the specific concrete events of history is an essential part of biblical thought, evidenced in the shift out of the early creation myths of Babylon and Egypt which were completely transcended by the Genesis concept of God's sovereignty, as well as the various accounts about David and Goliath, Daniel with Bel and the dragon, and even the amazing story of Shadrach, Meshach, and Abednego.

It appears that there is a constant tendency in man's nature which results in a flight from reality into fantasy, a retreat into the timeless myths of superhuman heroes who are able to conquer varying symbols of evil. The progression therefore from the shabby reality of the actual secret agent to that of the fantastic exploits in the Bond movies and their derivations might be expected to result in the even more unrealistic figures of Superman and Batman.

The test comes consequently when these extremes must be redirected back into reality and the daily problems of normal life. In each of many artistic attempts to depict the legend of St. George we can see how it was brought up-to-date within contemporary situations. As various artists projected their own conditions into the story we can find St. George depicted in different ways: as a noble Roman youth with classical beauty and strength, or as a valiant knight clad in an amazing assortment of clothes and armor and with the faces of different patrons who had commissioned specific works. By perceiving Fleming's representation of secret agent 007 as a contemporaneous St. George, we can accept his premise as far as bringing the image up-to-date. The most important factors are the dynamics of the action involved, not the clothes or the gadgets. It was just as anachronistic for the fourth-century martyr to be portrayed in the heavy armor of a fifteenth-century knight upon a white horse as it is for Fleming to have described him driving a fast car in a business suit.

By investigating the dynamics involved in images, we can begin to appreciate why it is inadequate to present an image of St. George alone. An image in itself can have great power. It can evoke action on both conscious and unconscious levels. Men may seek to imitate a hero figure by the unconscious mimicry of some ideal model, or they may deliberately undertake to act out a role. A little girl playing with her dolls illustrates the former, Don Quixote the latter. Neither way in itself is adequate, for the image then becomes either an icon or an idol. The factor of insight is missing, that fusing together of conscious understanding with emotional involvement, which produces commitment, will, courage, and action growing out of integrity. Fleming reflected some understanding of these dynamics, when he referred to Bond's "playing Red Indians" in the beginning of *Casino Royale* and when he stated at the conclusion of *Diamonds Are Forever,* "It reads better than it lives."

James Bond therefore in the role of secret agent 007 is not adequate to represent the image of St. George, not only because the movie version of his adventures has drifted so far away from Fleming's material, but also because these stories as fiction remain within the realm of myth or fantasy. In Marshall McLuhan's terms, Bond is a "hot image" and we need a "cool" one which is able to indicate commitment and complete involvement in depth. What we need is not the James Bond who was Fleming's original hero figure—a St. George in secret agent's clothing, nor the second James Bond who captured the attention of the mass audience, but a real-life figure in whom we might trace out the underlying dynamics of the image of St. George within an authentic situation in history.

In searching for such a person, we do not have to go very far, for there already is a man whose life and faith has succeeded in capturing the attention of a great many people. His story, which is fact, not fantasy, begins within our own century.

In July 1939, less than two months before the actual outbreak of World War II, a young German minister did a very peculiar thing to the distress of many of his friends and colleagues. Only a few weeks after his arrival in the United States for a speaking tour which they had arranged for his safety, he returned to Germany to face almost certain danger if he continued in his steadfast opposition to the Nazi regime.

At the time his action was relatively unknown outside of a small circle of international leaders in the ecumenical church movement and other theologians who had hoped that his life might be spared for the work of the church after the war. However, the letter which he wrote to Reinhold Niebuhr reveals Dietrich Bonhoeffer's own clear recognition of the necessity of acting within the immediate situation. In it he admits that he has made a mistake in coming to America:

> I must live through this difficult period of our national history with the Christian people of Germany. I will have no right to participate in the reconstruction of Christian life in Germany after the war if I do not share the trials of this time with my people. . . .
>
> Christians in Germany will face the terrible alternative of either willing the defeat of their nation in order that Christian civilization may survive, or willing the victory of their nation and thereby destroying our civilization. I know which

> of these alternatives I must choose; but I cannot make that choice in security.[9]

Although this letter may appear to indicate a turning point within Dietrich Bonhoeffer's life and ministry, it actually is on a direct line which could be drawn between his earliest theological papers and his ultimate execution in a concentration camp only weeks before the collapse of the Nazi regime.

The story of his life is one which Reinhold Niebuhr felt well worth recording in an article entitled "The Death of a Martyr" because "it belongs to the modern acts of the Apostles."[10] John Godsey has pointed out that Bonhoeffer was the "sort of person who, by his very demeanor, stood out in a crowd. There was a certain aura about this powerfully built man with aristocratic features and gentle eyes, which attracted people to him."[11] Martin E. Marty writes that only European theologians Barth, Brunner, and Bultmann and the two Niebuhrs and Tillich in America have been "more studied, invoked and analyzed than Bonhoeffer in the past quarter-century" (which means by really stretching a point we might term Bonhoeffer the 007 agent in theology!). There is little doubt that his life was marked not only by rigorous scholarship of merit and promise but also by a very clear application of Christian insight to the extremely precarious political situation in Germany during Hitler's rise to power and the outbreak of war. As a young minister he had presented a firm unequivocal opposition to Nazi policies from the very beginning. Only two days after Hitler's assumption of public office in 1933, Bonhoeffer gave a radio address which was actually cut off the air because officials recognized that he was making subversive indictments of the Führer principle by calling it a form of idolatry. From that time on, one by one the conventional channels for Christian witness were gradually closed to him. He was barred from teaching when he was thirty; from preaching at thirty-four; from publishing written material at thirty-five; and imprisoned at thirty-seven. Yet, as his close friend Eberhard Bethge points out, "each time this narrowing circle came closer, his acting and thinking gained power and stretched into new dimensions. When he was silenced for good at thirty-nine, he began to speak more loudly than ever before.[12]

In Bonhoeffer a strong Christian faith was confirmed by equally courageous action, yet constantly mediated by a warmth and concern for others. The witness which he gave not only in words but with his life has served to capture the imagination of both professional theologians and laymen. The fragmentary notes which he was able to smuggle out of prison to his family and friends are serving as a springboard for a whole new generation of theologians who are attempting to speak to the needs of what Bonhoeffer had termed the "world come of age."

There are several perspectives from which Bonhoeffer's life and writings may be viewed. The first approach is generally that of those who currently see him at the center of the intellectual labyrinth exposed by the "honest to God" movement. Martin E. Marty has pointed out that Bonhoeffer's broad appeal in this category cuts across many lines: "East and West, Protestant and Catholic, Liberal and Conservative, clergyman and layman, theologian and activist, Calvinist and Lutheran, across the ecumenical spectrum he has stood as a symbol," an appeal which goes beyond other reasons because Marty feels that Bonhoeffer "empathized with the newer kind of Christian believer and thinker, the dislocated, displaced inhabitant of a secular world."[13] It is this perspective which has been stimulated by Bonhoeffer's words, intrigued by such phrases as "cheap grace," the "world come of age," and the "non-religious interpretation of Biblical terminology," and therefore compelled to examine his writings for their relevance to current theology.

Yet Eberhard Bethge, the man who has known Bonhoeffer's most provocative writings best (*Ethics* and *Letters and Papers from Prison*) because he preserved and edited them for publication, might suggest a second approach. When asked which he considered more important, Bonhoeffer's life or his theology, Bethge replied, "Ah, that is a very interesting point. I think the two were closely connected, but I, since I am not a theologian, would say his life."[14]

It is within this perspective that we would point directly to the obvious moral and physical courage which Bonhoeffer displayed in joining the resistance movement against Hitler. In *The Rise and Fall of the Third Reich,* William L. Shirer has indicated how the vast majority of Protestant clergymen had followed orders to swear personal allegiance to the Führer, thus committing themselves both legally and morally to obey his commands. Just as the vast majority of German people had lightly given up their political, cultural, and economic freedom, most were willing to sacrifice their freedom of worship as well. As one of the members of the resistance group, Fabian von Schlabrendorff, observed, the "non-Nazis were almost worse than the Nazis. Their lack of backbone caused us more trouble than the wanton brutality of the Nazis. Many who had started as adversaries of National Socialism believed that, by swallowing successive doses of the new creed, they might escape the worst."[15]

As we have seen, Bonhoeffer had spoken out directly against the Führer principle from the beginning. He had also condemned the Aryan clause in which ministers of Jewish descent were forbidden to serve in the state church. Rather than serve in a German church under growing Nazi domination, in 1933 Bonhoeffer went to London where he ministered to Germans living there. At this time he had made the important contacts with such church leaders as Bishop G. K. A. Bell, the Anglican bishop of Chicester, through whom the newly organized Confessing Church in Germany could communicate with other Christians around the world. Although at one time Bonhoeffer had wanted to go to India to study Gandhi's principles of nonviolence, he soon realized the impossibility of retreating into pacifism and instead returned to Germany at the request of the Confessing Church in 1935 in order to direct the activities of several illegal underground seminaries. After the last of these groups had been disbanded by the Nazis in 1940, he then began his activities within the resistance group. Traveling under the cover of his employment as a civilian in the Military Intelligence Service, he was able to make several secret trips to Switzerland and Sweden in order to inform British church officials about resistance plans and to request their aid in contacting the Allied governments.

Once Bonhoeffer had become involved in what he had termed the "great masquerade of evil" in Germany, he explained his decision simply, "It is not only my task to look after the victims of madmen who drive a motorcar in a crowded street, but to do all in my power to stop their driving at all."[16] When the small group of conspirators was depressed in 1942 and inclined to postpone action, he revived their spirits by stating, "If we claim to be Christians, there is no room for expediency. Hitler is the Anti-christ. Therefore we must go on with our work and eliminate him whether he be successful or not."[17]

It is important to note, however, that even though his writings in his incompleted book on ethics reveal that he had already worked out the theological basis for his action, his decision was evidently a costly one. Bishop Bell reported that during their secret meeting in Sweden, Bonhoeffer was "obviously distressed in his mind as to the lengths to which he had been driven by force of circumstances in the plot for the elimination of Hitler." Although he was looking forward to an immediate coup d'etat, Bonhoeffer had said, "There must be punishment by God. We should not be worthy of such a solution. We do not want to escape repentance. Our action must be understood as an act of repentance."[18]

In addition to these reports, there is evidence from other men, who were unacquainted with his writings, which would point to Bonhoeffer's life as having represented a more signficant witness to his Christian faith. Although most of those who had been in prison with him were executed also, there is written testimony from two survivors, Fabian von Schlabrendorff and Captain S. Payne Best.

Schlabrendorff had been a member of the same small resistance group with Bonhoeffer and had stated that whoever had joined the group "had to realize that his life was doomed. A man's moral value begins only when he is prepared to sacrifice his life for his convictions."[19] It was he who had planted what turned out to be an unsuccessful time bomb on Hitler's airplane and then had had to recover it before its discovery. Although he had known that Bonhoeffer had been able to conceal their activities from the Gestapo when he was arrested in 1943, Schlabrendorff admitted his own shock when he saw Bonhoeffer in prison later on after his own arrest: "But one glance at his upright figure and into his eyes, radiating serenity and composure, assured me that the dangerous instant of recognition had passed without disturbing his habitual self-control." During the cold showers which they managed to take together, Bonhoeffer was later able to reveal to him how the Gestapo proceedings had been sheer blackmail:

> Outwardly he showed no emotion. He was always in good spirits, and invariably kind and considerate to everyone—so much so that, to my surprise, even his guards soon fell under his spell. In our relationship it was always he who remained hopeful, while I sometimes suffered from depression. He never tired of repeating that only that fight is lost in which you admit defeat. How often did he smuggle a scrap of paper into my hands on which he had written words of comfort and faith from the Bible.[20]

Captain Best, on the other hand, had never known Bonhoeffer before they met at Buchenwald in the prison camp. He had been a British intelligence officer, who had been kidnapped in neutral Holland by Gestapo agents and taken into Germany by force. When he reported his impressions during their last few days together, he contrasted Bonhoeffer with another member of the resistance group. The one, a militant churchman with the rank of a general, seemed "inclined to expect unquestioning obedience to his religious opinions," while Bonhoeffer was "all humility and sweetness":

> He always seemed to me to diffuse an atmosphere of happiness, of joy in every smallest event in life, and of deep gratitude for the mere fact that he was alive. . . . He was one of the very few men that I have ever met to whom his God was real and ever close to him.[21]

In describing the small worship service which Bonhoeffer had held for the prisoners on Sunday, April 8, 1945, Best said that he had spoken to them "in a manner which reached the hearts of all, finding just the right words to express the spirit of our imprisonment and the thoughts and resolutions which it had brought." Immediately after the last prayer Bonhoeffer was taken away by two guards, but before he left he had taken Best aside and said, "This is the end. For me the beginning of life!"

With these dramatic testimonies to his faith and courage, it would be very tempting merely to draw the obvious analogies between Dietrich Bonhoeffer and St. George. Just as the early Christian martyr had refused to worship the pagan gods at the emperor's command, Bonhoeffer refused to bow to the political expediency of his time. Bishop Bell had pointed out that Bonhoeffer was "one of the first as well as one of the bravest witnesses against idolatry. He understood what he chose when he chose resistance. . . . He was crystal clear in his convictions; and young as he was, and humble-minded as he was, he saw the truth, and spoke it with a complete absence of fear."[22]

However, we would lose the opportunity to understand the dynamics involved in the image of St. George if we were to focus separately upon either Bonhoeffer's writings or his activities. Although what he wrote and did are significant, they are the fruits of his faith and not the faith itself. Why he wrote and acted as he did is more important, because of his emphasis upon the whole man (the biblical view of *anthropos teleios*) and not the religious man (*homo religiosus*). Although he had observed himself that man was once again living in a time when reality had been laid bare, when once more there were villains and saints not hidden from public view, he had rejected completely the idea that Christ was calling men to be either heroes or saints: "To be a Christian does not mean to be religious in a particular way, to cultivate some particular form of asceticism (as a sinner, a penitent, or a saint), but to be a man. It is not some religious act which makes a Christian what he is, but participation in the suffering of God in the life of the world."[23]

By looking at both Bonhoeffer's life and his writings, we begin to get some idea of the interaction which went on between them, giving strength and vitality to his final words. Tillich once wrote that all theological statements should be made with risk and passion, but these feelings rarely come across on the printed page. As we read the last letters and papers which Bonhoeffer wrote in prison, however, theology begins to come alive in a special way and we begin to see what it really may mean to be a Christian in the twentieth century.

Although in his early works Bonhoeffer had presented very carefully prepared theological papers for the academic community, in his last writings we are given an opportunity to share in the process as he actually lives and works through his theology. We share in his loneliness for his family and friends especially at holiday time, in his desire to keep them from worrying over him, and in his affirmation that "people are more important in life than anything else." We participate in his concern for the terror of the young prisoners locked in their cells or lying on the floor in some insecure shelter during the recurrent nightly air-raids. We appreciate his attempts to maintain morale and his impatience with the sniveling propagandist and others who cannot contain their terror. Then we face with him his own admission of times of despair and fear, when he confesses to Bethge that everything in prison was really "too awful for words," and when he realizes that he has been putting on a theatrical show of being a "contented, cheerful, easy-going fellow."

But, more significantly, we begin to wrestle with the questions with which he began struggling: What is Christianity, and what is Christ for us today? How can Christ become the Lord even of those with no religion? What is a religionless Christianity? How do we speak of God without religion? How can we claim for Christ a world which has come of age?

These questions may be difficult indeed but, as Bethge has written, Bonhoeffer was never the "comfortable contemporary" or a "convenient analyst who addressed people from an easy chair." In addition, we may not consider his answers as conclusive, but only indicative of the direction he was taking. He admitted that they had come only at the end of the particular path he had traveled. Of primary importance, however, is the fact that he repeatedly insisted on speaking of God "not on the borders of life but at its centre" and rejected the use of God as either a working hypothesis or a *deus ex machina* who could be called on only at the end of human resources and perception:

> God cannot be used as a stop-gap. We must not wait until we are at the end of our tether: he must be found at the centre of life: in life, and not only in death; in activity, and not

> only in sin. The ground for this lies in the revelation of God in Christ. Christ is the centre of life, and in no sense did he come to answer our unsolved problems.[24]

Because of his faith that Christ takes hold of a man in the center of his life, Bonhoeffer offers us a deeper understanding of what it means for a modern St. George to face the problem of accidie. In his writings it is very clear that he knew that a man does not conquer this temptation by playing the role of a saint, but only through faith in the word of God. This problem was not just an abstract concern for him, however, but rather one of deep personal involvement. In the first letter which he was able to smuggle out to Bethge seven months after his imprisonment, he had written:

> You are the only person in the world who knows how often I have nearly given way to *accidie, tristitia,* with all its damaging effects on the soul. I feared at the time [i.e. of his arrest] that you must be worrying about me on that account. But I told myself from the beginning that I wasn't going to oblige either the devil or man—they would just have to lump it—and I shall always stick to my determination.[25]

The faith by which Bonhoeffer was able to resist this temptation of accidie was of necessity grounded in his own clear understanding of its nature. Many years earlier in a series of talks about various forms of temptation he had explained that in accidie the "grace and promise of God are attacked and put to the test. In this way Satan robs the believer of all joy in the Word of God, all experience of the good God." It is that form of despair about one's own personal guilt and of doubt in God's forgiveness, in which man's spirit rebels against the word of God, in which man demands an experience, proof of the grace of God. In accidie Bonhoeffer saw that man was "thrust by Satan into the highest temptation of Christ on the cross, as he cried: 'My God, my God, why hast thou forsaken me?' "[26] The weapon by which the Christian may conquer accidie therefore is a fresh understanding of the word of God itself, that in Christ's victory man has been called out of sin into a new life based on freedom and responsibility.

For Bonhoeffer there could be only one reality: the life into which God had called man through Jesus Christ. In his book on ethics he had proclaimed, "*'Ecce homo!'*—Behold the man! In Him the world was reconciled with God." In the really *lived* love of God in Jesus Christ he saw that the concrete message had been revealed once and for all, that the real world had been made the arena for man's activities, and that there could no longer be two separate spheres of life into which the sacred and secular could be divided. "But the whole reality of the world is already drawn in into Christ and bound together in Him, and the movement of history consists solely in the divergence and convergence in relation to this centre."[27]

One of the most persistent motifs of Bonhoeffer's theology, therefore, both formal and informal, was his emphasis upon "this-worldliness." In *The Cost of Discipleship* he discussed the implications of Luther's concept of grace in correlation to obedience:

> Luther's return from the cloister to the world was the worst blow the world had suffered since the days of early Christianity. The renunciation he made when he became a monk was child's play when he returned to the world. Now came the frontal assault. The only way to follow Jesus was by living in the world.[28]

Although Bonhoeffer places a consistent emphasis upon worldliness, it is important to note that he never meant a shallow worldliness based upon "cheap grace." He believed that the cost of making grace available to all without presenting a call to follow Jesus in the narrow way had resulted in the collapse of the organized church in Germany and that the word of "cheap grace" had been the "ruin of more Christians than any commandments of works." Discipleship within the world is not prescribed ahead of time. God did not confront the world with ideals and programs or by conscience, duty, responsibility, and virtue, but rather with his perfect love. Consequently the Christian must discard these rusty swords and instead seek the daily "conformation" with Christ as the Incarnate, Crucified, and Risen One: to be real man, to be sinner, and to be a new man before God. Biblical faith includes both the Old Testament understanding of a historical redemption (redemption this side of death) and the Christian hope which "sends a man back to his life on earth in a wholly new way which is even more sharply defined than it is in the Old Testament."[29]

In his concept of "this-worldliness" Bonhoeffer recognized that men would find themselves in a new relationship of maturity before God which might entail a feeling of "forsakenness." He suggested however that God "has been teaching us that we must live as men who can get along very well without him. The God who is with us is the God who forsakes us." For Bonhoeffer, the experience of the absence of God would never be the occasion to succumb to accidie or to proclaim that God is dead. For him, the absent God is the "beyond" who is in the midst of our life. As an antidote for a syncopated society, he would point out that in the polyphony of life, God is the *cantus firmus* to which the other melodies of life provide the counterpoint. For a long time Bonhoeffer said he had thought that he might acquire faith by trying to live a holy life, but later he wrote that he had discovered that it was "only by living completely in this world that one learns to believe."

> One must abandon every attempt to make something of oneself, whether it be a saint, a converted sinner, a churchman (the priestly type, so-called!), a righteous man or an unrighteous one, a sick man or a healthy one. This is what I mean by worldliness—taking life in one's stride, with all its duties and problems, its successes and failures, its experiences and helplessness. It is in such a life that we throw ourselves utterly in the arms of God and participate in his sufferings in the world and watch with Christ in Gethsemane. That is faith, that is *metanoia,* and that is what makes a man and a Christian (cf. Jeremiah 45). How can success make us arrogant or failure lead us astray, when we participate in the sufferings of God by living in the world?[30]

Because God has shown his love not for an ideal world but for the real world, Bonhoeffer stated that man may no longer worship the world nor flee from it into a religion based upon personal pietism or abstract metaphysics. Because God has shown his love not for ideal men but for real men, men may no longer set themselves up as judges over each other or devise ethical systems based upon abstract principles. Because Christ has affirmed all reality, man has been called out of sin into life under the Lordship of Christ as the "man for others," the man in whom we are set free for genuine responsibility. In explaining his concept of deputyship in his book on ethics, Bonhoeffer brings a completely theological perspective to bear upon the whole question of the self as agent. He pointed out that "not the individual in isolation but the responsible man is the subject, the agent, with whom ethical reflexion must concern itself. . . . No man can altogether escape responsibility, and this means that no man can avoid deputyship."[31] Bonhoeffer saw Jesus Christ as the origin, essence, and goal of all responsible life and believed that the responsible man is one who commits all of his action into the hands of God and lives by God's grace and favor.

Because he had recognized that the time was over when "men could be told everything by means of words," Bonhoeffer knew that it would not be abstract argument, but rather concrete example which would continue to give the words of the church emphasis and power. In his life therefore he has given us this witness and provided our generation with a concrete example of the image of St. George, pointing the way from religion into responsibility and from apathy into action which is centered always in Christ as the "man for others."

NOTES

001 INTRODUCTION: "SLUG IT APATHY!"

1. A. M. Rosenthal, "Study of the Sickness Called Apathy," *New York Times Magazine* (May 3, 1964), p. 24.
2. William Butler Yeats, "The Second Coming." Reprinted with permission of the publisher from THE COLLECTED POEMS OF W. B. YEATS. Copyright 1924 The Macmillan Company, copyright renewed 1952 by Bertha Georgie Yeats.
3. W. H. Auden, "After Christmas," *ibid.,* p. 468.
4. Harrison Salisbury, *The Shook-Up Generation* (New York: Fawcett World Library, Crest Book d775, 1958), p. 167.
5. Erik H. Erikson, *Insight and Responsibility* (New York: W. W. Norton, 1964), p. 227.
6. Quoted by Malcolm Muggeridge, *Esquire,* Vol. 62 (December 1964), p. 36.

002 "THINGS ARE NOT WHAT THEY SEEM"

1. Cf. the following books about Ian Fleming and James Bond:
   Kingsley Amis, *The James Bond Dossier* (New York: New American Library, 1965).
   Sheldon Lane, ed., *For Bond Lovers Only* (New York: Dell Publishing Co., Dell 2672, 1965).
   O. F. Snelling, *007 James Bond: A Report* (New York: New American Library, Signet Book D2652, 1965).
   Lt. Col. William Tanner, *The Book of Bond* (New York: The Viking Press, 1965).
   Henry A. Zeigner, *Ian Fleming: A Biography* (New York: Duell, Sloan & Pearce, 1965).
2. Cf. the following references:
   "The Bond Phenomenon," *Newsweek,* Vol. 65 (April 19, 1965), pp. 95-96.
   Russell Baker, "Observer: James Bungler, Mass Hero," *The New York Times* (April 15, 1965), p. 32.
   Jacques Barzun, "Meditations on the Literature of Spying," *American Scholar,* Vol. 34, (Spring 1965), pp. 167-178.
   Robert Harling, "The Ian Flemings," *Vogue,* Vol. 142 (September 1, 1965), p. 222.
3. Robert L. Short, *The Gospel According to Peanuts* (Richmond: John Knox Press, 1965).
4. Edgar Allan Poe, "The Purloined Letter," in *Major American Writers,* eds. Howard Mumford Jones and Ernest E. Leisy (New York: Harcourt, Brace and Co., 1945), pp. 759-760.
5. Quotations from the James Bond series used in this book are from the Signet paperback editions published by the New American Library of

World Literature, Inc., New York, except those from *The Man with the Golden Gun* which are from the hard cover edition of the same publisher. All subsequent quotations will be indicated by the appropriate abbreviation from the following key (copyright date follows title):

CR *Casino Royale* (1953)
LLD *Live and Let Die* (1954)
M *Moonraker* (1955)
DF *Diamonds Are Forever* (1956)
FR *From Russia with Love* (1957)
DN *Doctor No* (1958)
G *Goldfinger* (1959)
FY *For Your Eyes Only* (1959, 1960)
T *Thunderball* (1961)
TS *The Spy Who Loved Me* (1962)
SS *On Her Majesty's Secret Service* (1963)
YOL *You Only Live Twice* (1964)
GG *The Man with the Golden Gun* (1965)

6. *The Seven Deadly Sins,* foreword by Ian Fleming (New York: William Morrow, 1962), p. ix.
7. Quoted in "Bond's Creator," *New Yorker,* Vol. 38 (April 21, 1962), pp. 32-34.

003 DOCTOR NO REVISITED

1. Paul Johnson, "Sex, Snobbery and Sadism," *New Statesman,* Vol. 55 (April 5, 1958), p. 430.
2. John Canaday, "The Quiet Necromancer," *New York Times* (December 19, 1965), p. X 17.
3. Quoted in *Playboy,* Vol. 11 (December 1964), p. 100.
4. *Third Part of King Henry the Sixth,* Act II, Scene I.
5. *Richard the Third,* Act V, Scene III.
6. *Henry the Fifth,* Act III, Scene I.
7. *First Part of King Henry the Sixth,* Act IV, Scene I.
8. Christina Hole, *Saints in Folklore* (New York: M. Barrows, 1965), p. 32.
9. Quoted in *For Bond Lovers Only,* p. 19.

004 THE HOT IMAGE IN THE COLD WORLD

1. C. G. Jung, *Symbols of Transformation,* tr. R. F. C. Hull (London: Routledge & Kegan Paul, 1956), p. 303.
2. Martin E. Buber, *The Eclipse of God* (New York: Harper Torchbook Edition TB12, 1957), p. 119.
3. Cf. Kenneth E. Boulding, *The Image* (Ann Arbor Paperbacks, The University of Michigan Press, 1963). Also Daniel J. Boorstin, *The Image* (New York: Harper & Row, Colophon Edition, 1964).
4. Herbert Read, *Icon and Idea* (New York: Schocken Books SB105, 1965), p. 53.
5. As reported by Eric R. Wolf, *Anthropology* (Englewood Cliffs, N. J.: Prentice-Hall, Inc., 1964), p. 78.

6. Herbert Read, *The Forms of Things Unknown* (New York: World Publishing Co., Meridian Book M168, 1963), p. 101.
7. Norman Shrapnel, "The Literature of Violence and Pursuit," *Times Literary Supplement* (June 23, 1961), p. 387.
8. Arthur M. Schlesinger, Jr., quoted in the *New York Times* (November 25, 1965), p. 8.
9. Conrad Knickerbocker, "The Spies Who Come in from Next Door," *Life*, Vol. 58 (April 30, 1965), p. 13.
10. Cf. discussion by Joseph Henderson, "Ancient Myths and Modern Man," in *Man and His Symbols,* eds. Jung and von Franz (Garden City: Doubleday & Company Inc., 1964), especially pp. 112-113.
11. "Secret Agent Man," written by P. F. Sloan and Steve Barri, published by Trousdale Music Publishers, Inc., Copyright 1965. Used by permission.
12. Cf. Erving Goffman, *The Presentation of Self in Everyday Life* (Garden City: Doubleday Anchor Books, 1959). Also Peter Berger, *The Precarious Vision* (Doubleday & Company Inc., 1961).
13. John Le Carré, *The Spy Who Came in from the Cold* (New York: Dell Publishing Co., 1965), pp. 129-130.
14. *Ibid.*, p. 150.
15. Donald Hamilton, *The Devastators* (Greenwich: Fawcett Publications, Inc., 1965), p. 165.
16. Adam Hall, *The Quiller Memorandum* (New York: Pyramid Books, 1965), pp. 115-116.
17. Hamilton, *op. cit.*, p. 178.
18. Le Carré, *op. cit.*, p. 150.
19. Hamilton, *op. cit.*, p. 147.
20. Hall, *op. cit.*, p. 118.
21. Søren Kierkegaard, in Walter Lowrie, *Kierkegaard,* Vol. II (New York: Harper Torchbook TB90, 1962), p. 429.
22. Ernest Becker, *The Revolution in Psychiatry* (New York: The Free Press of Glencoe, 1964), p. 205.
23. Enrique Vargas, "The Jet-Age Malady," *Saturday Review* (May 29, 1965), p. 18.
24. *Ibid.*, p. 19.
25. Allan Wheelis, *The Quest for Identity* (New York: W. W. Norton, 1958), p. 72.
26. Viktor E. Frankl, *Man's Search for Meaning* (New York: Washington Square Press, Inc., 1963), p. 121.
27. Cf. Joseph Goldbruner, *Individuation* (University of Notre Dame Press, 1964), especially chapter 12. Also Esther Harding, *Journey Into Self* (New York: Longmans, Green & Co., 1956).
28. Paul Tillich, *The Eternal Now* (New York: Charles Scribner's Sons, 1963), p. 17.

005 THE DEVIL WITH JAMES BOND!

1. Lewis Carroll, "Jabberwocky," from *Through the Looking Glass* (New York: Macmillan, 1963), p. 13.
2. Quoted in *For Bond Lovers Only,* p. 36.
3. Ian Fleming, *The Diamond Smugglers* (New York: Macmillan, Collier Books Edition, 1964), p. 29

4. Quoted in *For Bond Lovers Only,* p. 17.
5. E. V. Walter, "Mass Society: The Late Stages of an Idea," *Social Research,* Vol. 31 (Winter 1964), pp. 391-400.
6. Wolf, *op. cit.,* p. 12.
7. *Ibid.,* p. 20.
8. Joseph Campbell, *The Hero with a Thousand Faces* (Cleveland: The World Publishing Co., Meridian Book M22), p. 391
9. Stanley Romaine Hopper, "The Problem of Moral Isolation in Contemporary Literature," in *Spiritual Problems in Contemporary Literature,* ed. Hopper (New York: Harper Torchbook TB21, 1957), p. 154.
10. Material concerning Asmodeus may be found in Maximilian J. Rudwin, *The Devil in Legend and Literature* (Chicago: The Open Court Publishing Co., 1931).
11. Denis de Rougemont, *The Devil's Share* (Washington: Pantheon Books, Bollingen Series, 1944), p. 18.
12. *Ibid.,* p. 46.
13. Morton W. Bloomfield, *The Seven Deadly Sins* (Michigan State College Press, 1952), p. 243.

006 WHERE'S THE ACTION?

1. Arthur Miller, "The Bored and the Violent," *Harper's* (November 1962), p. 51.
2. Karl Menninger, *The Vital Balance* (New York: Viking, 1963), p. 378.
3. Norman Cousins, as quoted by Menninger, *ibid.,* p. 375.
4. Robert Merton, *Social Theory and Social Structure* (Glencoe: Free Press, 1949), p. 189.
5. Robert MacIver, *The Ramparts We Guard* (New York: Macmillan, 1950), p. 84.
6. James Robinson, *The Problem of History in Mark* (London: SCM Press Ltd., 1962), p. 50.
7. Karl Barth, *The Doctrine of Reconciliation, Church Dogmatics,* Volume IV, 2, trans. G. W. Bromiley (Edinburgh: T. & T. Clark, 1958), p. 378.
8. Paul Tillich, *Systematic Theology,* Vol. III (University of Chicago Press, 1963), pp. 231-237.
9. Harding, *op. cit.,* pp. 283-284. See also Harvey Cox, *God's Revolution and Man's Responsibility* (Valley Forge: The Judson Press, 1965), pp. 37-51; Josef Pieper, *Leisure, the Basis of Culture* (New York: Pantheon Books, 1952), pp. 38-45.
10. Morris West, *Petrarch and His World* (Bloomington: Indiana University Press, 1963), pp. 200-213.
11. Karl A. Olsson, *Seven Sins and Seven Virtues* (New York: Harper & Bros., 1959), pp. 34-40.
12. James A. Pike and Howard A. Johnson, *Man in the Middle* (Greenwich: Seabury Press, 1956), p. 77.
13. Miller, *op. cit.,* p. 56.

007 FROM BOND TO BONHOEFFER

1. Dietrich Bonhoeffer, *Ethics* (New York: Macmillan Paperback Edition, 1965), p. 68.
2. Miller, *op. cit.,* p. 56.

3. Ian Fleming, *Thrilling Cities* (New York: New American Library, Signet Book P2694, 1964), pp. 77-78.
4. *Ibid.*, p. 119.
5. Gabriel Vahanian, *Wait Without Idols* (New York: George Braziller, 1964), p. 243.
6. H. Richard Niebuhr, quoted in Vahanian, *ibid.*, p. 52.
7. Geoffrey Chaucer, *Canterbury Tales,* modern English version by J. V. Nicolson (Garden City: Garden City Publishing Company, Inc., 1934), p. 594.
8. Lewis Mumford, *Green Mansions* (New York: Harcourt, Brace, 1947), p. 65.
9. Quoted by Reinhold Niebuhr, "The Death of a Martyr," *Christianity and Crisis,* Vol. V (June 25, 1945), p. 6.
10. *Ibid.*
11. John Godsey, *The Theology of Dietrich Bonhoeffer* (Philadelphia: Westminster Press, 1960), p. 13.
12. Eberhard Bethge, "The Challenge of Dietrich Bonhoeffer's Life and Theology," *The Chicago Theological Seminary Register,* Vol. LI (February 1961).
13. Martin E. Marty, *The Place of Bonhoeffer* (New York: Association Press, 1964), p. 14.
14. Quoted by Ved Mehta, "The New Theologians," *New Yorker* (November 27, 1965), p. 159.
15. Fabian von Schlabrendorff, *They Almost Killed Hitler,* as told to Gero von Schulze-Gaevernitz, ed. (New York: Macmillan Co., 1947), p. 11.
16. Quoted by G. Leibholz in Dietrich Bonhoeffer, *The Cost of Discipleship* (New York: Macmillan Paperbacks Edition, 1963), p. 28.
17. Quoted by G. K. A. Bell in *The Church and Humanity* (London: Longmans, Green & Co., 1946), p. 175.
18. *Ibid.*, p. 172.
19. Schlabrendorff, *op. cit.*, p. 137.
20. *Ibid.*, p. 138.
21. S. Payne Best, *The Venlo Incident* (London: Hutchinson & Co., 1951), p. 180.
22. G. K. A. Bell, in *The Cost of Discipleship,* p. 7.
23. Dietrich Bonhoeffer, *Letters and Papers from Prison* (New York: Macmillan Paperback Edition, 1962), pp. 222-223.
24. *Ibid.*, p. 191.
25. *Ibid.*, p. 84.
26. Dietrich Bonhoeffer, *Temptation* (London: SCM Press Ltd., 1963), p. 44.
27. Bonhoeffer, *Ethics,* p. 198.
28. Bonhoeffer, *The Cost of Discipleship,* p. 51.
29. Bonhoeffer, *Letters and Papers from Prison,* p. 205.
30. *Ibid.*, pp. 226-227.
31. Bonhoeffer, *Ethics,* pp. 224-225.